FUNERAL DIVA

FUNERAL DIVA
PAMELA SNEED

CITY LIGHTS BOOKS | San Francisco

ISBN: 978-0-872-86804-5

Library of Congress Cataloging-in-Publication Data

Names: Sneed, Pamela, author. | Scholder, Amy, editor.
Title: Funeral diva / Pamela Sneed ; Amy Scholder, editor.
Description: San Francisco, CA : City Lights Books, 2020.
Identifiers: LCCN 2020009381 | ISBN 9780872868113 (trade paperback)
Subjects: LCSH: Sneed, Pamela—Poetry. | Autobiographical poetry.
Classification: LCC PS3569.N34 A6 2020 | DDC 811/.54—dc23
LC record available at https://lccn.loc.gov/2020009381

City Lights Books are published at the City Lights Bookstore
261 Columbus Avenue, San Francisco, CA 94133
www.citylights.com

CONTENTS

HISTORY

Uncle Vernon was cool, tall, hazel-eyed, and brown-skinned. He dressed in the latest fashions and wore leather long after the 1960s. Of all of my father's three brothers, Vernon was the artist—a painter and photographer in a decidedly non-artistic family. To demonstrate his flair for the dramatic and avant-garde, his apartment was stylishly decorated. It showcased a faux brown suede, crushed velvet couch with square rectangular pieces that sectioned off like geography, accentuated by a round glass coffee table with decorative steel legs. It was pulled together by a large '70s organizer and stereo that nearly covered the length of an entire wall. As a final touch, dangling from the shelves was a small collection of antique long-legged dolls. This was my Uncle and memories of his apartment were never so clear as the day I headed to his apartment with my first boyfriend, Shaun Lyle.

It was the '80s, late spring, the year king of soul Luther Vandross debuted his blockbuster album, *Never Too Much*, with moving songs about love. If ever there was a moment in my life that I felt free, unsaddled by life's burdens, and experienced in the words of an old cliché, "winds of possibility," it had to be the time with Shaun Lyle heading upstairs to my Uncle's house as Luther Vandross blared soulfully out from the stereo, "A house is not a home."

Of course Shaun was not the first or last person with whom I'd experienced feelings or sensations of unbridled freedom. Like seasons, freedom came in cycles, like in fall, in college with no money, chumming around with my best friend and school buddy Michael. We spent late afternoons wandering Manhattan's East and West Village, searching for cheap drinks and pizza at happy hour specials, ecstatic in our poverty. Michael was a blond Irish Catholic punk rocker from Boston. We met when I was an RA at The New School's 34th Street dorms at the YMCA. They were narrow tiny rooms like closets and some floors served as a hostel for homeless men. Punk music blared from Michael's room. I would knock on the door commanding, "Turn it down." Eventually, we united over the fact he put a towel under the door to block smells of weed smoke that frequently leaked from his room into the hallway. Michael and I were both writers, astute critics, and teacher's pets. In fiction writing class, we formed a power block. No piece of writing done by another student escaped our scathing critique. Professors deferred to us. "Michael, Pamela, what do you think?" We sat next to each other with arms crossed. A student writer friend confessed to me later, "I was terrified of you two." We were obsessed with Toni Morrison. I will never forget the last lines of Toni Morrison's novel *Sula*, which Jane Lazarre, our fiction teacher, made us read out loud as a class together.

"And Nel looked up at the trees," said "Sula, girl, girl, girl, all the time I thought it was Jud I was missing, but it was you."

Jane's eyes welled up as did mine and the whole class cried. *Sula* was a story of women bonding and friendship and longing and loss. "It's a truly feminist novel," Jane would declare. Feminism was her favorite topic. She was a straight woman with kids. She had grey hair and admitted she smoked pot. She was so cool, she'd write things on the board and say out loud, "Oh, I can't spell."

Michael and I were both work-study students. We covered for each other. He would call me after a night of drinking and partying and say, "I just can't do it. I can't go in. Will you go?"

"Sure," I'd say.

One day Michael and I skipped school and hung out near the entrance of 72nd Street and Central Park West. I stared at a figure across the street in a café. "There she is," I said.

"Who?" Michael asked.

"Toni Morrison, and beside her is June Jordan," I said.

"You're crazy," he said. "No way. That can't be them. How can you see that?"

"Yes, it is." We investigated. Sure enough, sitting beside a low fence of the café was Toni Morrison with June Jordan in dark sunglasses. I approached. Michael lagged behind, astonished. "I love your work, Ms. Morrison," I said. At the time I wasn't such a huge fan of June Jordan. I'm not sure if the reason I disliked her had to do with the fact she had tried to pick up my girlfriend Cheryl while visiting/lecturing at The New School or perhaps I wasn't ready for her message. Knowing what I know now—if only I could go back through a time capsule and tell her how much it meant for me to hear her in person. Long after she would die of cancer and wrote the words in dialect "G'wan, G'wan!" telling us a new generation, to go on. Long before the collapse of the twin towers, before the massacre of so many gay men from AIDS, wars against Brown bodies in Iraq, Harlem, and Afghanistan, before the growing epidemics of cancer, rape, police violence, domestic violence, mass incarceration, depression, demise of our pop stars, she said to a class at The New School in the true form of a prophet, speaking of the U.S.: "This country needs a revolution."

Maybe it was June Jordan, like Audre Lorde, who taught me the power of what words could do. In retrospect, she opened the doors and flung open the windows to my consciousness, like when I heard Maya Angelou's poem, "Still I Rise," when I was nine years old. It awakened me. Just recently, with the terrible results of the

2016 presidential election, with Donald Trump elected, I can see June Jordan in sweet smiling profile, reciting as resistance, "Poem About My Rights."

Michael and I had many other adventures. We frequented Lower East Side Clubs like The Pyramid and The World. The Pyramid was a dive on Avenue A near Tompkins Square Park and famous for its vodka and lime specials; where some nights vodka gimlets were 2-for-1. One night I was asked to dance by a handsome young white-skinned man. I learned he was from Brazil. When the dance ended, I walked away.

"OMG," Michael said. "Who was that guy you were dancing with?"

"I don't know," I answered and shrugged.

"He's beautiful," Michael exclaimed. "Go back and get him." Michael had a thing for Latin men.

I danced back over. I yelled over the music, "My friend wants to meet you." I introduced him to Michael, and the rest was history. We learned he was visiting from Brazil and on vacation in New York for two weeks. It was his first time to New York. He spoke little English. He was bisexual. He and Michael had a two-week affair and fell in love. His name was Karim.

Six months later, after Karim had returned to Brazil, Michael and I were in Tompkins Square Park. It was the time right before they'd begun to gentrify the park. They started to impose curfews and later the police occupied it in a standoff with local residents. Michael and I were swinging on the swings. He had a container of beer masked in a paper bag. We were discussing Toni Morrison. Out of the blue Michael said, "I want to go to Brazil and get Karim."

"Sure," I said, just like that, no questions asked. We saved all of our money and six months later ended up in Rio. It was our first stop

4

in a month-long trip to Brazil. Our mission was to get Karim and bring him back to New York.

I had only ever been out of the country once before. In Boston while still at Northeastern University, I met Annette. I'd been invited by her to go with her and her family to Jamaica. It was an exciting and new endeavor getting my first passport. It was also exciting when I received the blue square document, too square and big to fit in my wallet. Annette was mixed-race, Jamaican born, with brown skin and green eyes. I was working with the African American Institute at Northeastern to assist in recruiting more Black students. I traveled to New York with a Black man who looked like Sidney Poitier. He was dark and very proper, from the Islands as well. We stayed at a high-rise, budget hotel on 34th St. It was far from luxury, but you could see buildings and some rooftops of New York City. From the window you could also see people bustling on the street below. It was hot, there was a steel beige air conditioner in our meeting room.

The pool of Black applicants came. I noticed Annette immediately, she was pretty and exotic. I didn't have a language then for attraction. Annette looked at me and shouted "That mole." She was referring to a prominent black mole on the left side of my nose, a beauty mark. Annette also had a mole in the exact same place. We bonded over our shared feature. Later, I'd notice former President Barack Obama also has a mole in the exact same place. I see myself in him, in his long elegant stature. I imagine sometimes, not knowing my origins, he is my brother. Annette ended up enrolling at Northeastern. We became friends. We were both pot smokers. Annette's appetite for it was much larger than mine. She stayed most days in a near coma. I suspected then she was hiding something, always numbing herself, but we never talked about it. She never talked about her feelings. I did learn something, which surprised me then, that she had a white boyfriend and expressed disdain for Black men. Still, she was fun in other ways and at the end of one school year, she invited me to Jamaica with her family. I was introduced to many new concepts. We stayed at a resort condo and her family had a cook and a housecleaner.

In Jamaica, I learned of and tasted many new foods like breadfruit, ackee, and salt fish. I was also introduced to a tropical climate and encountered for the first time the phenomenon of a flying cockroach. It flew through the air like a mutant ninja beetle. I heard of new names and places like Negril, and I went swimming in Dunge River Falls in Montego Bay. I tasted curry goat for the first time. I bought a large print dashiki and wore it to a family event and a beautiful dark Jamaican man stared at me. On the beach together, Annette and I met a young Jamaican guy who sold us weed and wove it into baskets to hide, unravel, and then smoke when we got home. This young Jamaican guy was also a delight to tourists because he knew how to eat or swallow light bulbs. I'm completely serious. The trip to Jamaica was life changing. The turquoise waters, the tropical air, the warm climate, winds blowing gently, the sun. I came to crave it all of my life; it was the very beginning of my wanderlust and appetite for freedom.

At the hotel in Rio with Michael, I was rereading Toni Morrison's *Song of Solomon*, which informs an unpublished memoir I wrote called *My Soul Went With her*. It is titled after Winnie Mandela's memoir *Part of My Soul Went with Him* written in the apartheid years when she and her freedom fighter husband Nelson are separated, and he has gone underground to evade capture. *Song of Solomon* uses the mythology of the African runaways who could fly, but my story is based on a mother who left trying to escape an abusive marriage and me imagining as she takes flight, runs away for freedom, part of my soul goes with her. I imagine for all slaves left behind, forced into separations, part of their souls too went with the runaways, the dead, and the lynched. I imagine a character in Chimamanda Adichie's, *Half of a Yellow Sun* set during the Nigerian Biafra war, and a traumatized mother carries her dead son's head by hiding it in a calabash. Besides the stories of the Africans who could fly, what I remember from *Song of Solomon* was the character Hagar, who had fallen in love with Milkman, who decides if she couldn't have his love, she would have his hate. I also remember the character Pilate, Hagar's mom, who wears a hat and sucks straw through her teeth. She is mostly silent, but when Hagar dies, she breaks her silence, walks into a church, and screams out, "Mercy, I want Mercy." That scene is resonant today, as so many Black mothers have to bury their children prematurely because of police and state violence. It's like our collective grief as a people is being expressed. Trayvon Martin, Emmett Till, Mike Brown, Sandra Bland . . . We are all Pilate and the real life Mamie Till in 1955 looking into the coffin of her murdered fourteen-year-old son, his face battered beyond recognition shouting up to the rafters, "I want MERCY."

Karim met Michael and me in Rio. Initially we weren't sure if he'd even show up. He was traveling from his residence in Brasília. While waiting in the hotel, I serenaded Michael with Nina Simone songs. Michael always shook his head appreciatively when I did this. "You're Nina," he'd say.

Michael spoke Spanish and it helped us navigate the Brazilian Portuguese as both languages are closely related. In the first few days, Michael and I watched the sunset on a beach in Rio. We were obsessed with caipirinhas and the beach at Ipanema as we'd heard it in the song, "The Girl From Ipanema." Though Michael was a White Irish Catholic punk-rocker and I, a 6' 2" Black girl who'd grown up in the church, he and I like lovers had begun to resemble each other, had sifted into each other like sand.

There was a funny moment between us when I noticed that all the women on the beach in Rio wore G-strings and bikinis and I wanted one. We went to a bikini shop. I tried on a G-string and stepped out of the dressing room. Michael's face turned flush red. "My god Pamela," he said, embarrassed. "You look amazing," but I noticed he was shy to look.

When we were giving up on Karim and left the hotel for dinner one night, we saw Karim walking toward us. We reunited and spent weeks travelling around Brazil. Karim took to us to his home. It was a city nothing like I'd expected Brazil to be. We spent a few nights there snorting pure cocaine. Instead of making you speedy, it made you numb. Whitney Houston was popular at the time and every five minutes she played on the radio. The announcer yelled excitedly, "And Whitney Houssssson," omitting the T.

Our trip was successful; months later Karim relocated to be with Michael. He enrolled in film school. During this time, Michael and I eventually outgrew each other, but moments of freedom came again and again, like the summer I spent with a lover, wearing Gucci sunglasses and her driving a Mercedes convertible through North Carolina's back woods and hidden roads, imagining paths slaves once traveled, pursuing liberty. Top down, wind behind us, her one hand on the steering wheel, other in mine, we felt contented as we listened to hip hop sounds of the reigning soul priestess Mary J. Blige. In a piece I wrote called *Motherland and Chitlin Chimichanga*, I imagine the intersection of Latin and African American culture, the presence of Black blood all over America. In the past now and forever there is Black blood.

"In North Carolina looking at trees in a forest, you can still taste, smell, and feel remnants of Black blood. Driving past newly rekindled and restored plantations you can still imagine crimes that occurred, imagine hierarchies that defined us for centuries, house niggahs, field niggahs, overseer and master."

The main character of *Motherland* is a designer from North Carolina searching for her Black identity, who would, like me, become deeply impacted by the AIDS crisis.

There are ways I've come to crave Blackness like never before
search its eyes for some semblance of me
a way I watch Black shows on television
listen to the rhythm of our speech endless amounts of shucking and
    jiving
a way I've studied those Black male musical singing groups like the
    Temptations
fascinated by steps we've devised
a way I watch young Black & Puerto Rican girls on the block near
    my house
the way they've fastened gold to their ears, wear name belts
I saw this young Black girl sashaying down the street the other day
in a shirt that looked like the American flag
the way I hear the clipped and musical patois of West Indian women
and want to call some of them mother
the way I need to watch how our hips curve
our bodies move perfectly when we dance
the way I've gone to some offbeat dance club
on a rare occasion and heard someone playing drums along to the music
then an updated disco remixed version of Patti Labelle's "You are
    My Friend,"
and me getting the holy ghost
feeling as if it was early 1991 all over again
all my brothers were still alive
they really all didn't just die on me
I really did belong once to somewhere, something
and no matter how much I grow, attempt to move on

I never stop thinking of never stop missing those men
their hands
beautiful Black hands
hands that shaped America's soil
Black hands
unseen hands
creative forces
purveyors of style
masterminds who've made much
of music and fashion what it is today
Black Black beautiful hands
working like miners in the mines of South Africa
like slaves to whom I owe almost everything
men like nameless and tireless women
working every day in the country sides and fields of Nicaragua and
    Mexico
Those masked fighters those men, like women and girls barely
    bloomed
once called them Sandino's daughters
who risked everything to fight in a war against dictatorship
went against tradition left their families, everything
to create futures for their children
beautiful, Black Black queer hands
I know I'm just a designer
I shouldn't know and feel all of these things
but I do read do travel
and Sebastian says, I could make a great leader.

On the topic of freedom and runaways, there was a winter, a
whole season spent with a lover. We drove her beat up Volkswagen
to escape the city, like runaways hiding out upstate at a bed and

breakfast for ten dollars a night. We did nothing except eat, make love, and hold hands as we stared into a warm fireplace.

Years later, long after I first began to pen this story, I travelled to Ghana and met Joshua. He was twenty-one years old. He was my guide. We sat on a hilltop overlooking the beach, and kissed as he blew weed smoke into my mouth. Someone rode a bicycle on the wet sand. In Ghana, Joshua and I traveled up to Aburi Gardens, its tall trees formed a holy corridor. Afterwards, we sat in the red dirt waiting for a tro-tro, a dilapidated mini-van, and shared a bushel of small bananas. From the paths near Aburi Gardens we could look out over all of Accra and see tin roofs and tiny hills.

There weren't many words between Joshua and me. Perhaps we both wanted pieces of each other's identity. We were from very different cultures. When I wanted to run an errand, he'd say things in the popular phrase, "Go and come," which meant finish your business, come here, stay here and be with me, but we did share a common language when we packed and boarded the tro-tro. He negotiated prices with the driver in Twi or Gha. We held hands as we sped by images of Ghanaian fields. We were silent. Joshua took me to the beach at Kokrobite, outside Accra and we'd swim. We were somewhere in the hills in Burkina Faso, it looked the way you'd imagined Africa, tropical, with large palm leafs.

In a small hot room, he tore my bra off and we fucked. "I like your sex," he'd say, which was his way of saying he liked the way I moved with and beneath him.

There were times, too, with Joshua when the outside disappeared and it was just he and I in a room somewhere in West Africa fucking. There was a time too when it got serious, after I'd left the first time. He would call me and say "Come home." He knew that for African Americans there was a wound there, a wound that had us searching all over Africa for an identity, a place to belong. As a guide, I wonder

11

if Joshua was trained to know there was a wound in me, that in general for African Americans home was a fractured place. Time after time he'd seen the desperate looks in African American eyes, those mythologies about Africa being a homeland that made us bend down and kiss the tarmac when we arrived. Maybe there was something Joshua knew when he took me for the first time to Cape Coast Castle, the slave fort. I am not a religious person, not into ancestral worship, but I went immediately to the water banks near Cape Coast and began to anoint myself with water and pray. Joshua knew to be silent and watch.

For those who haven't seen Cape Coast Castle, it is a slave fort, the dungeons or warehouse where the British and Portuguese first held sugar and then slaves, thousands of them before being shipped to the new world, parts of the Caribbean and America. There are slave forts all along the coast of West Africa, just as plantations are lined along the Mississippi. In Ghana, Cape Coast is among the most famous and a huge tourist attraction. It's a huge sprawling castle and underneath are dungeons where slaves were held. There are different dungeons for male and female slaves and rebels. They are dark, dank rooms where a guide points out fingernail scratches in the wall where captured Africans clawed to get out. The guide also points to the window high above where food was dropped down into the dungeon where slaves stood knee deep in vomit, feces, and urine. In the last part of the tour, you are shown The Door of No Return, where you look from the dungeons onto the Atlantic ocean. Once slaves stepped through this door, they would never see their homeland again. Maybe Joshua knew a lot more than what he actually said when he took me weeks after Cape Coast to an African Village for a naming ceremony to receive my African name. It might have been a heist and a hoax gone wrong, because I was supposed to receive my name in a little ceremony, pay and go, but when they dressed me up in African garb, and the Village gathered around me and the Village priestess said, "Thank you God for returning our daughter from across the ocean," and said to me, "You are home now, you will never be a stranger and sleep in a hotel again," something in me like rock split apart. I started to cry as did she and we couldn't stop.

I know Mandela used to do that—embrace African Americans. In a simple gesture he extended his arms and said, "Welcome home," and that embrace could make men weep. I do believe contrary to all intellectual beliefs, there is something spiritual in returning. There is something that happened to my soul, making that zig zag trek across the ocean. There is something about being a survivor. There is something in my D.N.A. There is something monumental at least there was for me, standing in Cape Coast Castle, looking from The Door of No Return onto the Atlantic Ocean. There is something about seeing the first leg of our real journey and the enormous ocean we crossed.

Like Alex Haley in the film *Roots* and finding his people, I resisted every urge to throw myself down on the ground and shout, "I found you," with all the tears and snot and the holy spirit jerking my body all around like the way it did to church folks. There is something about passing through these huge, newly constructed gateways, memorial arches on a beach in Ouidah that symbolize The Door of No Return, and next to it, The Door of Return, like arms extended to all of those descendants of slaves dispersed into the diaspora. It was part of Kwame Nkrumah's dream, to unite a fractured and broken Black people. There is something, too, that made me feel victorious, that despite all odds we have triumphed. As Audre Lorde once said of women, of lesbians, of POC, "We were never meant to survive," but we have and thrived. Like many, I never expected to feel anything at Cape Coast, some don't. Some think it's a tourist trap, but it changed me. In fact if my life were divided into halves, I would label them pre- and post-Ghana.

I had stayed in Ghana for one month. Hurricane Katrina in New Orleans happened while I was away. I watched horrified from a hotel room on television how a tidal wave of water rushed through a building and trapped a young Black woman in the basement. Her head bobbed up and down, she gasped for air. I also saw while staying in the hotel a film about organ harvesting and poor people who are tricked into selling their organs for profit. The film starred a young British actor of African descent Chiwetel Ejiofor who would go on to become the star of the American film made by a British director, Steve McQueen, *Twelve Years a Slave*. The hotel played the mini-series *Roots* on rotation, about Kunta Kinte captured from his African homeland and sold into bondage as an American slave. In this way, the hotel was peddling to tourists an identity, or a nostalgia for the past, creating connections where there may be none. Many Black Africans do not consider African Americans to be their family or long lost tribe and actually resent this type of thinking.

After meeting and traveling with Joshua, I returned home. My worldview had changed considerably. The first film I saw upon returning was the remake of *King Kong*. It was offensive to me, the fact that Hollywood would adapt and release a film with very racist origins. Though couched in science fiction, it was about a Black man (a monster) who was infatuated with a white woman, Naomi Watts as Faye Wray. In 2005, this film was regressive. I was appalled as were several Black men in my neighborhood who saw it. I decided to write a satire as a protest of that film titled *Kong*. What I saw after returning from Ghana was Kong's voyage, stolen from Africa, lured, drugged with chloroform, chained, made a slave, loaded unto a ship, a journey from his homeland through the middle passage to America. "This Kong," I wrote, "you want to be free." What became evident to me was not only the racist caricature and configuration of white men's fear, but Africa's displaced and missing son.

The only saving grace for Peter Jackson's *King Kong* was that Kong was not just a racist fantasy or byproduct. He was resurrected in a post 9/11 world. In Peter Jackson's *King Kong*, Kong is an American soldier, handling business in the jungle. He works on behalf of justice. In the famous scene where he is shot down from on top of the Empire State Building by ironically tiny planes, we are meant to see America's vulnerability. He is the American people, a Great Goliath being slain by the young David. Kong is America's innocence.

When I left Africa for the first time and returned four months later, Joshua had become a man. When we first reunited I teased him and asked, "Where's my little boy?" I saw his shirt sleeves rolled up, the muscles and veins in his arms strong. We were in a room with a thatched roof, on the beach next to Cape Coast Castle, the slave fort. "Come here. Move here. Be with me. We can travel," he said. "Travel," was the word that got me. I was tempted by the idea of leaving everything behind, going with him, traveling, but I was ultimately just passing through. "Your eyes don't say forever," he'd say. I'd quickly look away as if caught.

At the beginning of this story, I spoke of Shaun Lyle, whom I met in the season of Luther Vandross's "Never Too Much." In the end, he doesn't qualify as a real boyfriend, but he was a first for me. I'd known him long before he'd ever noticed me and long before that fateful night we kissed on a balcony overlooking the city. I'd already spotted him. I was a freshman in junior high school and he was a senior. Like spring, Shaun arrived late in high school years. The first time I spotted him he stood outside on the top steps of my school. He wore a fashionable brown tweed tailored suit, which was uncustomary and sophisticated for a student in our small town. His face was turned away in profile smoking a cigarette. He resembled the

15

Romans or a Greek God, a bronzed statue you'd see turning pages of an ancient history book, face turned away in profile with a sharp European nose, only Shaun was Black, mixed-race, with caramel skin, hazel eyes, and hair a mosh of soft brown ringlets. He hadn't noticed me, but I'd noticed him and his beauty. I was deeply desirous and promised myself, one day he'd know me.

In fact, from that day forward, I went out of my way to walk downstairs in the high school to the ground floor near senior lockers, hoping to catch a glimpse of him. I prayed our eyes would meet and truly he'd see me. Besides being in different classes, we were in different leagues. I'm sure in his eyes I was some gangly young freshman, no one who could be of consequence and merit to him. So based on these facts, neither of us could have guessed he'd be the man introducing me to destiny, would be the vehicle I drove and ultimately arrived at myself. He was my introduction to a new world.

Shaun was *that* beautiful, but he had problems that had to do with family and history. There were scandals and rumors that preceded and followed wherever he went. His family, the Lyle's, were the most notorious of our small town and surrounding ones. Some of the problems had to do with his mother, who was also beautiful, a white porcelain-colored Black woman with the elegance and chiseled features of an Egyptian Nefertiti. It was suspected she was addicted to prescription painkillers, often in car crashes, and spent months out of work, living like a reclusive heiress. She seemed interested in men only for what they gave and had the erect posture of a kept woman. I felt there was something incestuous between Shaun and her, never actualized but an uncomfortable union. There was also his sister Roberta who'd been in and out of jail, notorious for hooking up with criminal men. Then, there was Shaun's slightly younger brother, Scott, who might have been beautiful, but in stark contrast to his flamboyant family, was remote and lifeless. Shaun, in his early twenties, had been in and out of jail, which was the reason he'd never finished high school and had to go back. He rarely talked about his past, but these were the rumors surrounding him, mystery that created fear of him and his entire clan. I heard his father shot someone.

So, perhaps the Shaun I'd met after our brief visual encounter on the high school stairs was a young man trying to redeem himself, trying as hard as he could like a prisoner or slave to break away, escape from family and the air that surrounded him. Perhaps he was attempting to master his own destiny by going back to finish high school and attending the same church as I did, where his grandparents were prominent figures. Perhaps church was his very public attempt to turn his life like a vehicle around, to gain the acceptance he and his family had never had.

On the day he and I officially met, he was sitting in church with his back to me in a front pew. It was a Saturday rehearsal for baptismal candidates, people who had in very traditional terms accepted Jesus as their savior and were willing to follow the path of Christianity. I have no idea what caused me to be baptized. I can only say it seemed like the thing to do. I was moved one Sunday (as much as I was moved hearing Luther Vandross) when the preacher extended his arms and asked the congregation as he did every Sunday, "Won't you accept Jesus as your personal savior?" There was something very theatrical about it all for those like me, numb to the ways of Christ, when the floorboards opened, the pulpit moved, and you stepped into a shallow pool with a preacher fully clothed in white robes, who dunked you into the water.

However, I was now eighteen years old and a high school senior. I was also thinking about plans for the prom. I was certainly not the first pick as a 6-feet-2-inch tall, dark-skinned Black girl amongst white boys. Prospects for a good prom date were slim. I had asked James, someone's cousin of a cousin, but as time grew closer, I explained to my cousin Lisa that Saturday in church, "I'm not so sure about the prom because James is waffling in his answer." Perhaps it was spring and I had purposefully planted information, because it was right then that Shaun turned to me and said, "It would be an honor to take you to your senior prom."

No one and nothing could have prepared me for the most beautiful man I'd ever seen volunteering to take me to my senior prom. I can't tell you to this day or in a thousand years what motivated Shaun to do this, if it were his newly reformed sense of Jesus and desire to do a good deed, if he'd wanted to rectify himself in the eyes of Jesus or the church, or if by some remote chance he'd seen or witnessed in me some possibility of beauty, a beauty which escaped eyes of my small town, parents and boys alike. Perhaps Shaun saw potential in my tall, gangly form.

It was soon after I loved him. I loved him hard and became one of a string of women who loved him, though I was definitely the youngest and most naïve. The rest were porcelain, older, green-eyed, and glamorous like his mother.

There was something soft and magical he'd awakened in me the night of my senior prom. I was dressed in an ivory gown, he was in a tuxedo. We stood late night on a balcony. He kissed me openly and gently. Afterward he informed me, quite officiously, "Let's see each other," which like a late spring night was a cool way of saying, Let's date, but by no means be exclusive. "Sure," I said, playing cool while my heart nearly exploded. Perhaps I'm skipping around now as I did then, but I don't remember any fear when sometime after the prom, in early summer, while riding in the backseat of a car with Shaun as someone else drove, he lifted my pant leg from the bottom and stroked his fingers up and down like a paintbrush effortlessly. Like a light bulb my skin prickled with electricity.

My mind flashes and races to the first time in his apartment above his grandmother's. We were not fucking but he's naked as I lie beneath him, topless, whispering into his ear breathlessly like a radio, turned on. In the end, he sits naked, back propped against the pillows, muscular arms and legs folded looking like those pictures of the Romans or a Greek God, only Shaun is smoking a cigarette. I stand at the edge of the bed in full view getting dressed. His eyes like the lens of a camera surveys my body and breasts. Though it's my first time naked with a man, somehow I am unafraid to show myself. Like an artist or sculptor Shaun looks at me appreciatively and says, "Your body is beautiful, Hun."

It was through Shaun that I was introduced to new ways of life. Everything about Shaun and his family was illicit. He took me from church and the suburbs into the back roads of Boston, which led like steps to an underground scene. Like the leader of a band or great conductor, Shaun took me to the first parties in Boston among artists and actors who starred in famous controversial plays, lived in kooky, alternative, and communal households. These were artists who had living rooms like my Uncle Vernon, decorated for effect, but instead of antique long-legged dolls, they displayed larger than life-sized wooden crosses and a huge stereo speaker system. These were artists who ran toilet paper through the streets at night as a signal and trail to the party. They also displayed ambiguous and diverse sexuality. They looked at my stature and shouted appreciatively, "Amazon, Amazon!" These were artists who weren't afraid to take God's name in vain. There were men who wore black leather jackets with tassels on the ends that jumped up when they danced. These were Black artists who dropped acid and were children of famous New York authors. These were Black artists who attended boarding schools, were students of the elite Harvard, Black artists who stayed in areas of Boston that are now too prestigious to live in.

Shaun introduced me to the underground Black gay sections of Roxbury, Dorchester, Mattapan, and to the infamous Thayer Street—the artistic loft section behind the drunken men's hostel, where artists lived when it was still affordable. It was also at the height of the punk era with debuting bands like The Violent Femmes, Psychedelic Furs, and the Butthole Surfers. Shaun introduced me to Black gays who threw Friday night parties on Thayer Street. Everyone dressed up like on Halloween in dramatic costumes and stayed up all night waiting in anxious anticipation for the moment when Chaka Khan's mega-hit "Ain't Nobody" blasted through the speakers. At the party's end, in a stunning dénouement, the other campy disco hit would blast out, about a scorned woman who comes to say to her lover, like Jennifer Holiday in the Broadway hit *Dream Girls*, "It's not Over." The entire place would go berserk with people dancing and living it up. These were artists who waited for Friday night to buy eight balls of cocaine and did it in back rooms where only the coolest of cool were invited. With Shaun I was always invited. His beauty and charm like my own were passports to a new world.

Eventually, Shaun faded into the background. I joined a vanguard and moved to the fore of an artistic world, which became my family and a trail leading me out of my small town. Through Shaun, I gained courage to call myself a lesbian, and it was he who showed me the pathway to becoming an artist.

Shaun was not gay, but gays were his chosen people. He prided himself on being different, and men as well as women loved him. There were trysts and things he'd never mentioned, like his father having shot someone, and he himself having spent time in prison. Sometimes it seemed like a cross he carried like Jesus.

One day in early summer, I had run into Shaun in downtown Boston. We stood on cobblestones near Boston Commons. We were newly broken up. We weren't speaking. I was angry. "Hey Hun," he said, charmingly, "Come to my birthday party," he said. "I'd like you to meet my new lover."

I can't tell you what made me say yes, but I did. We all met in Shaun's tiny apartment above his grandmother's house. She was blonde with one side of her head shaved. I wore a white leather miniskirt. I'm not sure what he told her about me, but she burst out in declaration as if to counter anything he'd told her, "She's beautiful." We all ended up at the house of probably another woman Shaun was seeing. He disappeared into a backroom with her to do drugs while Lauren and I sat in the living room, chatted, and fell in love. She introduced me to punk music and a punk lifestyle. Most of her words were, "Fuck this." I remember early on sitting in a diner with her and she threw sugar packets across the room at people. She was rude. She taught me to eat bananas and chocolate with coffee, and that dessert could come before a meal. She broke rules.

In the way that Joshua changed and became a man when I returned to him, I became a woman with Lauren. I changed overnight. It was my love for her that made me stand up and challenge my father.

On one particular eve, I was going to meet her. I was ironing my clothes, a light blue man's shirt. My father was lying on the couch, drunk and angry, noticing all the changes in me and said, "You're not going out, you're not to leave this house."

"Yes, I am," I said.

"You're not," he commanded. Our fight escalated. He had a history of violence against women, his wives, but never with me. "Look at you, you're a goddamn lesbian," my father yelled. "You're wearing men's clothes." He was referring to all the ways my style had changed after meeting Lauren. The fight continued to escalate. He followed me into my bedroom and shoved me hard into the window. The large glass pane broke and formed jagged edges. With one sudden or false move, I might have fallen out or been sawed in half. But I fell forward. As I lay on the floor my father kicked me furiously in the stomach. That day, I left my parents' house and never returned.

21

After Shaun and Lauren, and moving to New York, I met Cheryl.

Cheryl was short, light brown, stocky, athletic and middle class. I was tall, elegant, working class from the suburbs. I pretended I was tougher than I was. I swore a lot. Moving to the city from Boston, I might as well have had a cow and a pail. I was that naïve.

Cheryl and I were opposites. She was introverted. I was extroverted. She was perceived as a good girl. I was perceived as a bad girl. I suppose we both needed some of what the other had. We met at the same YMCA on 34th St. where I met my best friend Michael. Cheryl and I became lovers. At the time she was dating a man and I know I must have seemed like Shaun to her—bold and beautiful, an out lesbian. There was a fear of me, too. Cheryl and I moved in together and we were each other's first lesbian relationship. We were able to consummate in a way Lauren and I did not. We were two Black women in a white school, and we negotiated that terrain together.

When I think about Cheryl there is a lot I don't want to talk about. There is pain and betrayal. At the beginning of our relationship I had gone with Cheryl to meet her brother. We both assumed we were playing it straight, keeping our physical distance, but later Cheryl's brother confronted her. "She's your lover," he said. He could tell in the way we moved together.

People have asked who I was at this time. Flipping through a journal I kept during those years, I read page after page that I felt numb. I numbed myself through partying. Michael, my new best friend, would call me at all hours of the day and night and ask me to go party. I always answered the call.

Of the two-and-a-half years we spent together, the end was the most important part with Cheryl. I'd outgrown the relationship, but I couldn't leave, coming from where I'd come from, having been orphaned as a child, it was unspoken that you never left someone. If you want to understand me, want a window into circumstances that shaped me, watch the film *What's Love Got to Do With It*, loosely based on Tina Turner's abusive marriage to Ike Turner, an abuse she eventually overcame. Return to the film's beginning, go to Nutbush, Tennessee, and meet a boisterous little child singer named Anna Mae Bullock. In the film's first scene she is a rebellious child singing in the church. In the second, she is being left by her mother, who is trying to escape an abusive marriage, which also happened to me. In a scene that exists in almost darkness, little Anna Mae asks her grandmother in utter bewilderment, "But why did she leave me?" The grandmother, unable to respond with any viable answer says in an effort to comfort, "Just don't you worry about it." In the third scene, Anna Mae is eighteen years old, reuniting with her mother and sister. She is resentful for having been abandoned. She meets Ike Turner in a nightclub and they share a love of singing. Later in the film, he renames her Tina.

Being left by her mother is the event that forms the basis of Tina Turner's marriage to Ike Turner. After the initial honeymoon, for years afterward, she is kicked, beaten, stalked, and raped. I believe no matter how monstrous Ike was, even if she were raped and beaten, she never wanted him to feel as bad as she had growing up, to feel that alone. She never wanted him to have the experience of what it felt like the day her mother left. It's worse than what a prison can do.

There's a scene near the end, after Tina has escaped. Ike surprises her in a parking lot. "Dammit," he says through the car window, "I want you to stop all this foolishness, Anna Mae, and come home."

He doesn't say Tina, the name he gave her, but appeals to Anna Mae, the little girl who was abandoned.

So it is because of this little or large happenstance in childhood, being abandoned by a parent, through years of abuse, you'll stay, through rape, the disparagement of your name, acid burning, scars . . .

Every day, your role is perfected, having been punched, beaten, kicked in the chest, threatened, thrown downstairs. It's happened so often it becomes a dance or a routine. As seniors, my parents adopted a wild little black cat. They named her Mysti but I've nicknamed her Bat Girl. She climbs up walls, shelves, breaking things, she tears the kitchen curtains going after a fly. She is also incredibly sweet and stays with me when I make art. When I'm at my parents', most of the day is spent with them asking, "Where's Mysti?" And we collectively search the rooms and under the beds to find her. I've nicknamed her Bat Girl because she was so wild as a baby that they kept her in her carrier with the door locked at night, and sometimes during the day, too. Most animals fear or dislike carriers but my mother's cat returns to it, sleeps there now as an adult willingly because it's where she finds comfort. She is unaware it's a cage.

Recently, I read the novel, *The Underground Railroad* by Colson Whitehead. The heroine is a slave named Cora, who survives almost everything, years and years of abuse. To survive she has to kill a man. Cora is also abandoned by her mother, who ran away from slavery and later dies from a snakebite. Cora survives a brutal rape on the Hobb plantation by a group of men. She is stitched up by other women on Hobb. Finally after a lifetime of being on the run, a runaway, she finds love, like the character in Lynn Nottage's play *Ruined*, where the main female character who saves other girls is also ruined but finds love. Cora's first instinct is to apologize to her lover about her rape. He says no, it is she who is owed the apology. The scene makes me think of what I have carried, things that I blamed myself for. It reminds me of Sethe, in Toni Morrison's *Beloved*. She can't stop mourning the child she killed to protect from slavery. The child haunts her and then finally disappears. She says to her lover Paul D, with deep regret, "She was my best thing." Paul D responds

with tenderness in the famous lines, "No girl, you your best thing."
"Me?," she cries and asks. "Me?"

Yaa Gyasi's historical fiction novel *Homegoing* starts in Ghana at Cape Coast Castle, and follows generations of slaves, symbolically cursed women and some men, Each of them carries a small stone around their neck, an heirloom passed between generations. Finally, in contemporary times, a young descendant is swimming with her male lover near Cape Coast Castle. They have returned as tourists. She takes off the stone her family has worn for centuries across generations. She tosses it to her lover and says, "Here, you take it." It makes me cry because finally she is free and no longer needs to wear the stone.

So I stayed with Cheryl, doing drugs and hurting myself. I always carried with me that little voice, like Anna Mae asking in darkness, "But why did she leave me?" Because I had been left by my first adoptive mother, because I had barely seen her again, because nothing was ever explained to me, I couldn't do to someone what was done to me.

One night while I was working at a bar, I left to buy drugs. Or, as I see it now, I was two people and one took me to buy crack. I went to the Lower East Side. Someone led me into a hallway. It was set-up. They saw I was green, alone. Attempting to get away, we struggled and stumbled out into the street. One said to another group member, "Give me the knife." Someone planned to stab me. I had a beautiful brown leather knapsack with my poetry from school. I realized in that moment that I couldn't give it up. Writing and what I had learned in Jane Lazarre's class was the only reason I had to live, so I fought.

I said, "Here, take the money, take the money," the hundred dollars or so I had in tips from bartending, but I wouldn't let go of the knapsack and the poetry inside. I somehow escaped, I don't remember how I got home. I took a long bath; I tried to scrub off what felt like dirt. I didn't tell Cheryl about the attack. After that night, and being confronted by Cheryl about drug use, all I could manage to say is, "I want to go home."

I boarded a bus to Boston, to my parent's house, but I misunderstood. The home I cried out for was not my parent's house, but a warm place in me. I was still sick in my heart from the attack, but I sat in my parent's house under a dull lamp light, reading to heal. I read Toni Morrison's *Beloved*. I got to the place where Sethe, the runaway slave, is found near dead in the woods. It's winter and she has frostbite. She is numb all over. She is found by a poor young white girl who massages her frost-bitten limbs. It's agony for Sethe. The young white girl understands and says, "Anything dead coming back to life, hurts."

From that moment on, like in the classroom at The New School reading *Sula*, my feelings came alive, all those that I'd repressed, and I started to cry. I thought of Baby Suggs, in *Beloved*, an aged grandmother who is also an unofficial preacher. In a clearing in the woods she tells slaves, in efforts to heal them, "I want you to cry now, for the living and the dead, just cry."

Later, in my twenties, after moving to New York to pursue education and life as an artist, long after Cheryl, Shaun and I stayed in contact. I returned to Boston for a visit. I was hurting from a break-up. I'd spent one of my school semesters drugging until it had gotten out of control. I think I'd called Shaun because in many ways he was still home to me. When we got together he took me out for old time's sake, for a night of snorting cocaine inside the loft of a famous photographer. I had visited the loft before, and was always impressed by its cool, the people, light bulbs and flashing cameras. We stayed up all night, Shaun, the photographer and me, drinking, snorting and smoking cocaine laced with PCP. By morning the room spun in my head. I could see glimpses of gray light through a covered window. Shaun was high and while readying to leave, he mumbled, "Listen, Hun, my car's broken down and I need some help to get started. My mom's working temporarily around the corner, and I'll go ask her to help us out with some money."

So he left, with no intention of returning. Meanwhile, I was being pressured by the photographer to perform a sexual favor in exchange for cab fare, which I needed to get home.

I remember a beautiful white cotton model's dress that the photographer instructed me to put on. It was sheer and beneath I felt naked and afraid. I remember the sour taste of a condom breaking, cum in my mouth, and a feeling of dirt and violation by both him and Shaun.

For a long time after I didn't speak to Shaun, or confront him for leaving me in that situation. I returned to New York, knowing there was no one in Shaun to confront, no conscious person who might have shown up and said, Yes, I love you, I'm sorry.

I began to realize that part of Shaun's mystique was his elusiveness, an ability to scheme women, while stringing along as many as possible. I suppose now, after traveling the world and living my life as an artist, I've met hundreds of Shauns, people who heap damage on you and act as if it never happened.

After many years, I contacted Shaun again. It was a few days before Christmas, and we met outside of his grandmother's house by an ornate tree. I had long since resolved the situation in the photographer's loft for myself. The Shaun who greeted me was not the same person I'd known. He was no longer the bright light leading me like a great conductor into a new world. His features were the same, same as the chiseled Nefertiti he resembled, but the sun that bronzed him was gone. I knew he'd been defeated by the same history and tragedy that surrounded his mother, father, brother, sister, and him. He could never escape.

"I was in the hospital," he said. "Had a car accident, broke a lot of bones and was self-medicating," which was his euphemistic way of saying, "I've been on drugs." I saw that he was suffering. I told him about my life in New York and my own current struggles. I wanted to show him how much I had grown up. He looked at me and said, "You're still so beautiful, Pamela. Please don't ever give up." And for one brief moment in the moonlight on a Boston rooftop he held me, with his lips brushing mine in quite the same soft way they had on prom night years before, when he'd awakened something in me . . . to longing, lust, and my power as a woman. So when he kissed me there and then, and held me in that moonlight, though what we had was far behind us, I felt my heart flutter for him, as it always had, beyond reason.

EPILOGUE:

Uncle Vernon passed away a few years ago. From my earliest memories as a child, I remember his painting and collages. He was the first person to ever plant in me the idea that anyone could be an artist.

My family has healed many things, some not. My stepmother is obsessed these days with the idea of me coming home . . . The other day she sent me a text out of the blue:

Hi Pam
I bought you a blanket and a comforter, so you won't be cold this winter when you come home.
Love Mom

Years later, I'm writing, performing, teaching. I still struggle with the aftershocks of abuse. As I finish this story, I am thinking of changing the title from ~~History~~, *instead dedicating it to all the Anna Maes of the world and calling it: For Me, Tina Turner, and All Black Women Survivors.*

ILA

THE LAST TIME I'd heard my true birth name was in Boston, when I was back in town partying at a gay club. I must have been twenty-seven years old when this beautiful caramel-colored butch appeared. She walked up to me and said cruisingly, "What's your name?"

"Pamela," I answered, haughty and full of New York attitude.

"Oh," she answered, disappointed. "I thought you might be this girl I knew once named Ila."

Shocked that anyone outside my family could have known that name, I shouted at the top of my lungs, "It's me, Ila," ecstatic to hear my birth name.

"I'm Marion," she said. "Remember, you hung out with my brothers, Troy and Tony?"

"Oh yeah," I said laughingly, finally making the connection.

Silently, I marveled to myself at how Marion, once a tomboy, a little sister, had grown into the handsome butch who stood before me. I also marveled at how she survived the small homophobic Massachusetts town we'd grown up in.

"You don't still live there?" I asked.

"No, no, I'm in college. Well," she said, walking away, "Nice seeing you again, Ila."

It's difficult to explain my name change, to say I was born under another name and had a different identity. It's difficult because the story involves not just me, but my family, primarily my father and his second wife, who thought changing my name was a good idea.

"Ill-ahhh," my fifth grade homeroom teacher, the red haired and mustached Mr. Mastriani pronounced laughingly (Ill-ahhh sounding like killahhh minus the K) for the entertainment of my fifth grade class.

"Ila not Ill-aahh," I said correcting him. I think he'd done that more than once, pronounced my name incorrectly for the benefit of the class. It was a technique designed to keep me in line, because of all the fifth grade girls in his class, I was the most boisterous and outspoken. His mantra was make a joke of the kids first, before they make one of you.

"Ill-ahhh-Sneeze," the fifth grade boys called me, embellished with a "ka-chew" for sneeze. "Ill-ahhh, the jolly green giant, and Hey Stretch," they said, probably because at age eleven, I was already 5'10", towering above my classmates. As if imagining I existed at a different altitude, they yelled "How's the air up there?"

In fifth grade I had wanted to fit in, belong, in size and shape and attitude to look like the girls in my classroom. They were all white, with varying shades of blonde, brunette, and occasionally red hair. There was Laura, dark haired and Jewish, and Robin, a raven-haired beauty. There was Marlene, and her younger sister who was severely pigeon-toed, whose parents spoiled them. There was Terry, an Italian girl whom we kids visited after school and whose mother was famous for making something called, "sauce." There was Deborah with long strawberry blonde hair, whom I taunted and put gum into her hair, which resulted in her having to cut it. They were all monstrously good. I, on the other hand, was dark-skinned, Black and unruly.

It was in fifth grade, the year that my name changed when I'd started acting out. I rebelled, talked back to authority, bonded with boys, and tried as best I could to make teachers like Mr. Mastriani miserable. I also terrorized the French teacher Mr. Blanch who wore a blonde toupee and made us conjugate verbs in rhythm. He would say, "*Répétez, s'il vous plait,*" and then bang his ruler on a desk for us to keep time like a drill sergeant. "*Un deux trois quatre cinq six sept huit neuf . . .* " I led the disruption with fart noises, paper planes, passing notes, and frequently got tossed out. In fifth grade, around my name change, is the time I'd secretly begun to tear my hair out in patches and chew strands. Fifth grade is the time I began to have bald spots and needed to wear a wig. It all began in fifth grade, when my name was changed.

As far as I know, I was born into the world as Ila Levette Sneed. The surname came later. This is as far as I know because for child adoptees, birth certificates are fictitious. They never reveal the mother's or father's name, nor the precise hour and exact location of the child's birth. These important facts are intentionally left out, stored in sealed records in government offices for the purpose of protecting and insuring the anonymity of the birth parent's identity. I can only assume my birth mother named me, having no other gift to offer. She named me "Ila," a special name for a girl she'd have to give away.

Yes, Ila is uncommon, and rarely if ever in my adult travels have I heard of anyone called by the same name. I presume it was my birth mother who named me, but maybe not. Perhaps in the adoption agency where I'd stayed for two years until adoption, I had a special friend. Perhaps it was like in a made-for-TV movie, when a nurse or social worker befriended me and named me "Ila." Perhaps the name Ila was a gift bestowed upon me for what they sensed would be an extraordinary human journey. I have no factual information about that time. As far as I know, life began with my father, the man who adopted me, and his first wife Ruthie, both of whom were and are to this day secretive about my origins.

It was reported to me by my stepmother, whom my father married after Ruthie, that upon meeting me at two years old, I'd run up to him in the adoption agency and said, "Daddy," flung my arms around him, though he was at that time a complete stranger. Something about me must have clicked for him also, because I was the one out of all the children in the world he picked. My father has never told me any of this history, and if it were up to him, I wouldn't even know this much. He never wanted me to know of my adoption, nor of life and history before him. It was my stepmother who told me.

"I know you think he's your father but he isn't, and Ruthie isn't your real mother." I was standing in the mouth of a long hallway that connected the kitchen to the bathroom and bedrooms in our apartment. I was six years old, speechless, and trying to piece the story like broken shards together. I was shattered, and had no way to understand it all. "If it weren't for your father and I, Ruthie would have sent you back to the adoption agency." Ruthie and my father had divorced two years previously. I understand now that my stepmother was jealous of my relationship to Ruthie. I understand now in a twisted battle for custody and ownership, she wanted to destroy any ties I had had to Ruthie.

I had lived with Ruthie for a short time after she'd divorced my father, and I'm hard pressed to believe she'd have sent me back to the agency. But as a six-year-old hearing that terrible news delivered and undisputed by anyone, I believed what my stepmother told me, which she finalized by saying, "Don't tell your father I told you. He wouldn't want you to know."

If I could physicalize how that news hit me—of my father not being my father and Ruthie not being my mother—I'd describe it as a crushing blow that sent me reeling into another stratosphere. Suddenly at six years old, the world I understood, thought was mine, was no longer true. I no longer belonged, nor had the key fundamental figures that any child needs to survive, a mother and a father. These facts were further verified by the fact that after my father remarried, Ruthie never came around, never rescued me as I'd always prayed she would.

My stepmother and I used to play a game of sorts, when my father went out; she would rifle through the paperwork in his top dresser drawer, looking for information about my identity. She came back one day and announced, "Your mother was 5' 10" and your father was 6' 4". She was light brown and he was dark-skinned. Their last name was Mills. He played basketball. They were from Virginia, but they came to Boston as students. They were young, that's why they gave you up."

It was top secret information. I had no way of verifying if what she said was true, but I held onto those descriptions for the rest of my life. If the analogy was drowning or trying to survive, their names were a raft tossed to me. Also, she said, don't ever search for them; it will kill your father.

There are two significant stories I must tell, both are important to my identity, and both involve waiting. Before my father met my stepmother and remarried, he was a single parent, a young man who wanted to play the field. For these reasons and also while he worked, my grandmother, his mother, Pearl, often babysat me. Once or twice a year, at school there was a PTA night where teachers gave interested parents in-person progress reports. I had been so good in kindergarten, I had the capacity to write and spell long before the school taught me, because of my father's at-home lessons. He would sit me down at a table and teach me the alphabet. I copied him as he wrote out I-L-A. I know how important this was to my father, who didn't have a high school diploma.

I could not wait for my father to go to the PTA night and for teachers to tell him how good I was. But the evening of the meeting he was on a date. In the living room of my grandmother's house was a huge rectangular picture window. From it I saw down to the end of the street, the Daniels school park with the small hill we kids sled on during winter. I could see the solitary tree on the hill. As we grew up it was the tree we sat under and shared deep conversations, experienced a first kiss. From my grandmother's window, I saw the entire side of Daniels elementary and junior high school. It was a red colonial building with a long Lego modern wing attached. Beneath my grandmother's window was an old fashioned silver radiator. On the eve of the PTA meeting I perched my five-year-old self on the silver radiator, like an owl on a branch. I sat and stared out and looked for my father. Hours passed, my father never appeared until finally the school lights started to go out. Every time a light went out in the elementary school and then the junior high, disappointment fell onto my shoulders like two ton bricks. When my father finally arrived home, he was drunk and my grandmother, who I'd rarely seen angry towards him, said in a low voice, "She waited for you all night, why did you do this to her?" I couldn't hear his response.

The other significant event which shaped me involved waiting for Ruthie, my first mother. Unlike on a PTA night, the waiting wasn't contained to a few hours or an evening but extended decades, almost a lifetime. Ruthie had dark brown skin and moles that covered her face like freckles. She worked at a beauty shop. She was a hairdresser. In the fashion of many African American women of her time, she wore silver bangles that went up her arm almost to elbow, and were collected from different and exotic places like Barbados, Jamaica, Trinidad. Once on a trip to Bermuda after she and my father divorced she bought me a silver bangle like hers, which she instructed should never be taken off. I was so impressed at that age of being able to be like my mother and having a bangle like hers. Eventually though, the bangle which I did take on and off, bent and was lost.

When my father first remarried, Ruthie stayed in contact. There were gifts, occasional cards, but eventually without warning or explanation they stopped coming. I knew that I shouldn't ask why. So, I sat down by the window like the same little girl perched on a radiator on a PTA night and waited for my mother.

For the seventeen years I lived in my parent's house, I sat often in front of the window on the corner of my bed and dreamt I saw Ruthie, my mother coming up the drive to rescue me. Pretty close to my eighteenth birthday I realized Ruthie would never appear and that dream like lights in the elementary school on PTA night long ago, faded. I suppose the final nail in the coffin of my relationship with Ruthie came when my stepmother confessed without guilt to having burnt all of my baby pictures, pictures of Ruthie and me, which attested to life before her.

My name and how much I disliked it was the only thing my stepmother ever paid attention to. When I came home in 5th grade complaining about teachers and boys calling me, "Illaahh," for some reason she listened. Truthfully, I did not dislike my name, and she could have explained to me then the power and beauty of being different. She could have told me that honoring my name would be the first step in a courageous and lifelong journey. She could have held me as social workers and parents did in those PBS after school specials about troubled teens, and she could have said, you're special my dear and your name is part of who you are. Someone, somewhere a long time ago loved you very much to give you a name like Ila.

Instead my stepmother said, "Let's change it. Let's change your name," and that's when we took on the project of searching through baby books for a new name. It was something we did together, and I suppose in retrospect that I was also desperate to be my stepmother's daughter. Desperate to have her regard and pay attention to me, to be the daughter she dreamt of having with my father, to be that pretty girl who would surely have been light-skinned and caramel-colored with good hair, who would have been good, unlike me who could never seem to fit in, fly straight, or win her love and approval.

We were sitting in the familiar place, her on the couch, and me on the brown recliner. It's a choice, she'd said, after narrowing down hundreds of names in the baby books, between Pamela and Leslie. I wavered. "Leslie," I said. "Les-lee," I said sounding it out like some student in an ESL class, but for some reason Pamela had the ring of a princess. "Pamela," I said. "I want my name to be Pamela."

From that day forward, my name was made official in the courts, I underwent a name-changing ceremony, and my stepmother was officially named my legal guardian with her name added to my fictitious birth certificate. This is primarily how the story ends, with me becoming Pamela, and leaving my name like a country of birth behind. Sometimes I think of changing it back, but Ila is dead. I've grown up and formed an identity as Pamela—a poet, performer, teacher—but every so often I think of my name and my mind drifts to a girl I met in college, a white girl named Ananda, whose family and she were forced to leave South Africa during the apartheid era. They were exiles who lost everything coming to America and I remember every time Ananda spoke of her homeland, her eyes welled up with tears, throat croaked with longing.

I disliked Ananda. In every class I challenged her, "How can you only speak of yourself, your maid named Beauty, and the land you left behind when every day Black people fight and die for basic rights." The white teachers coddled her, pulled me aside after class, said, "Leave her alone, she's not on your level." Now I look back and every so often like the fruit and guava of Ananda's homeland I miss Ila, I miss that little girl, I miss my father calling me Ila on every occasion up until my eighteenth birthday, almost as if he couldn't help it. He never fully accepted the name Pamela. It was the way he understood me and what made me his.

I miss my aunt and grandmother calling me Ila, pronounced with a Southern twang which sounded like Allah, substituting the I sound for an A and drawing out the first A so it sounded like God. "Alllaaah," I'd hear ringing out from the front door of my grandmother's house Allah come here.

"Yes Ma'am," I'd say, answering back respectfully. Perhaps this is why I was so happy in the gay club when that girl called me Ila. It was the last time anyone who knew me then called me Ila, like someone from a different era, and I received it like a gift, a special part of home and a secret past only a few can attest to.

Epilogue:

Recently I took a group of students on a class trip to Nuyorican Poets Café in New York City. A middle-aged, brown-skinned Black man approached and asked, "Are you Pamela?"

"Yes," I said, thinking he was a stranger. Instead, he was a second cousin I hadn't seen in more than thirty years.

"It's me, Reese," he said. "I knew it was you."

For a moment the part of me I thought dead came back.

He said again, "I just knew it was you, Ila."

FUNERAL DIVA

During the '80s, that seemingly idyllic time when
men men girls girls
I was part of a Black lesbian and gay movement.
I don't know how or where it came from
but a lot of us found ourselves in New York City moving
from small town safety
outer boroughs and families
with hopes of discovering the big apple.

At this time, great Black lesbian warrior poet, essayist,
and foremother Audre Lorde was a living entity
like pioneering Black gay author James Baldwin, she gave voice
to an identity once shrouded like a widow behind the veil of secrecy
    and silence.
And it was Audre Lorde alongside James Baldwin whose fighting
    and words
birthed a generation of somewhat nameless travelers
into what I have titled unofficially as a Black lesbian and gay
literary and poetic movement.

It was the year 1986 when Other Countries, a literary troupe
for Black gay male writers formed.
In 1989, I had just finished college and had begun to make my name
as a Black lesbian poet.

A young, impressionable, and burgeoning star, it was natural
I gravitated toward Other Countries
reminiscent of the '60s Black Power Movement
I saw each collective member as a brother.
In return, I became their sister.
At the time, I also worked at an agency for lesbian and gay youth and
was becoming what is called a prominent figure
Like a job which requires: wardrobe, good politics, poetry,
but above all willingness, readiness, and ability to speak
and speak I did.

As activists and founders of a new social and literary movement,
busy writing, publishing, building foundations and networks
to employ future generations, while changing the society we knew,
we were oblivious and unprepared when in the mid-'80s
a devastating and unexplained phenomena struck, eventually called
    AIDS
like new homeowners watching a whirlwind tornado
destroy dreams of home, camaraderie, and friendship
Like the recent Black populous of Katrina and Haiti
through hurricanes and earthquakes
saw pillars, foundations, and platforms they'd built washed away
but in our generation it was young Black men who like babies
or children had just begun to articulate, voice thoughts, ideas and
    desires
that never in the world's history been spoken,
dying as soon as, moments of, or seconds after
pressing pen to paper.

These were early days, AIDS in its infancy,
before the medical establishment invented drug cocktails

providing life support and badly needed medicine
without which men could and did die within weeks, months of, or
shortly after diagnosis.

At this time, as in the '40s during World War II
when men enlisted, went abroad to become soldiers,
while women at home were drafted into the work force and
   professional realm,
took on untraditional roles as welders and electricians
like banks but instead lent limbs, additional hands, and
the occasional missing shoulder.
Because of my stature, writing, outlandish outfits, and flair for the
dramatic
I became a known and requested presence operating throughout the
   crisis
as an unofficially titled, "funeral diva," called for
at memorials, readings, wakes and funerals to speak
give testimony and credence to men's lives
even if they were not family members or close friends
like a job which requires at such sudden, rapid and rising death tolls
quick thinking
like wordsmiths who can articulate at mathematic speed,
capture within hair's breath, bottle the essence,
execute like marksmen small and mundane details,
all the while like members of the clergy or great actors having the ability
to accurately portray and pay homage to the spirit of someone
who'd lived only for a short time on this planet.

Armed with only a few pre-requisite experiences:
As an adopted and only child, weathering my parents' divorce
Later, a beloved grandmother, my shelter and protector

devoured by cancer
turned from a robust brown woman to a small gray thing
who could not recognize me
At the funeral, in tribute each of my cousins wore the feathered and
    veiled hats
of her favorite church collection.
At the memorial for Craig Harris poet, activist, and soldier
I was prepared.
Craig worked tirelessly on the frontlines of the AIDS epidemic at
    GMHC,
Gay Men's Health Crisis,
But in off hours between battling KS and pneumonia
and trips to the hospital,
he drank champagne and smoked long Virginia Slim cigarettes,
famous for the slogan aimed at women and their transition from
    skirts to pants
announcing on billboards "You've come a long way, baby."
A true rebel and pioneer Craig vowed in one of his poems about AIDS
Not to succumb gently, but defiantly, insisted, like a generational star
"I will go out like a fucking meteor."
For his work at GMHC, Craig talked passionately about AIDS work
in Harlem at a time when illness and gayness was taboo.
To those who would oppose and refute him, he said humorously
"Honey, I've got a few bricks in my pocketbook which I'm not afraid
to throw."
Later at a memorial and tribute to Black lesbian poet Pat Parker
who died of cancer
Craig asked in vigilance, way ahead of his time,
acknowledging women in a voice resounding over the auditorium
at the Gay and Lesbian Community Center on 13th Street, in a
    poem about

the massive casualties of AIDS and those left behind,
"Who will care for our caretakers?"
a question that still resonates today as I think of Black women poets
whose words like hands, shoulders, arms were used to uplift
whose eyes like stars in darkness provided vision
led us like runaways to freedom
whose poems, songs, and spirits were used to eulogize,
bury dead,
make sense of senseless tragedy.
They were teachers, nurses, soldiers, working long hours
mostly without vacation or pension plans, retirement or a leave of
    absence
like Harriet Tubman who provided years of service
to Union soldiers and received little pay, walked away empty
like soldiers returning now from Afghanistan and Iraq without
    services or beds
to sleep on.
Many died silent invisible deaths from cancer with no one to care.
These were the women Craig spoke of when he asked,
"Who will care for our caretakers?"
After a long ferocious battle with AIDS, like a gladiator
or Viking warrior made famous by Kirk Douglas, Craig did succumb.
At the memorial as tribute similar to when my grandmother died
I wore a large circular hat with swirling orange and blue circles
reminiscent of a '40s, '50s style movie star diva
Craig loved and emulated.

For Rory Buchannan, a poet and activist, who juggled many roles,
as a father to a teenage son while holding down a full-time job,
was also a member of Other Countries and GMAD, Gay Men of
    African Descent,

at the wake, I had no words to express my love and gratitude
   towards him
for hours we spent like musicians and secretaries at keyboards typing
my first poems, then his own and organizing them into respective
   chapbooks.
We sat in his living room one afternoon making up famous quotes for
our book covers, comparing ourselves humorously with stars of the
   time
like Audre Lorde.
Rory was spiritual and when first diagnosed with HIV, he believed herbs
could heal him.
In the kitchen, there was a crockpot with warm smells emanating
all day through the house.
Death's swiftness caused in all of us, such accelerated
insight and poetic gems
lines from Rory's poem still play over and over in my head
like an old 45
"I stopped looking for Mr. Right when I found out I was him."
At his memorial, like bottles of fine wine broken open to celebrate
between friends, I read a poem of mine that he loved when
I rewrote the story of Rapunzel and portrayed her not
as a blond woman pining for Prince Charming
but as a liberated Black woman with dreadlocks.
"That castle," I said, "was the love she and the wicked witch built,
and she did not need any rescuing."
In closure, I imitated the way I'd seen my grandfather and
   grandmother
and church elders use bible quotes, but instead I used the refrain
of an old R&B classic and vowed like a younger sister gazing up
at a protective older brother in reverence I sang

imitating the voice of the great baritone of the late soul singer Barry
    White
"No matter how I high I get, I'll still be looking up to you."

Months later when David Frechette, one of Other Countries
first members, died, I was not able to attend the funeral
but like a legacy between the business of wakes and funeral as comfort
I often repeated to myself lines of his famous poem, titled
after the song by French chanteuse and diva Edith Piaf, "*Je Ne
    Regrette Rien,*"
a song in which David adopted the lyrics into his own language and
Black gay experience which states in English, I have no regrets
lyrics which seemed to articulate not just my feelings, but the mood
of a generation.
He wrote: Sister Chitlin and Brother Neckbone
gather around my deathbed asking me to repent
The wicked ways which brought me here
But I don't regret hours spent in arms of world-class insatiables
Or the hunk I made love to prior to a Washington March
Though my body be racked with fevers and pains "*Non, je ne
    regrette rien.*"
And it was these simple lines like lyrics that challenged the sadness
    and shame
accompanying AIDS, stigmas, and misconceptions that said
gays caused their own illness
these lyrics which challenged the fear and temptation to wallow
in self-pity by spitting back, "*Non, je ne regrette, rien.*"

I'm not sure where it belongs, but I must insert:
there were times when I, the Funeral Diva, was not always noble,
I was traveling while my dear friend the visual artist Don Reid was dying

and I ran away.

We worked together at the Hetrick-Martin Institute for Gay and
  Lesbian Youth.

He was an art therapist and at twenty-three years old I ran the
  afterschool program.

I met him on a panel first at Harlem Hospital.

He was part of the group that existed in the '80s called
Black and White Men Together.

At that panel, Don carried on his back the baby son he'd adopted
with his white partner.

This is long before gay people adopting children was common.

His son's name was Max, and he was a tiny brown baby Don adored.

Later, working at the Institute, Don and I would have many
  adventures
and escapades with Baby Max in tow.

There was a time a year or two after Max started walking, he wanted
to be a peacock for Halloween.

Don being a gay man, a visual artist, and sudden costume designer
searched day and night for real feathers.

He spent all night sewing together Max's costume.

There was also a time we took Baby Max to church and because
Don raised him to be free, Max wandered down the aisle at three
  years old,
stood next to the preacher and did an interpretive interpretation of
  the preacher's
words.

The preacher seemed annoyed, but Don, a proud parent smiled
the whole time.

I remember our offices at the Institute
located on the Westside Highway, across from Hudson River
and infamous Piers.

There was lots of sunlight.

We were in formation.

We were making ourselves.

While others were dying around us, Don was in denial about HIV/
AIDS

We never talked about it.

Even when he got the tell-tale pneumonia, the rapid weight loss,
and the terrible fear.

We never said AIDS.

By then, I had left the agency, I was traveling as an actor and
leaving the next day when I heard Don was in the hospital.

I understand he asked for me.

I heard his voice in my head asking a friend, "How's Pam?"

But my feet were leaden, I couldn't go.

I didn't want my last image to be of a man shrunken down
to a skeleton.

Like the recent survivors of Hurricane Katrina and Maria in
Puerto Rico,

I was grief-stricken and waterlogged.

Maybe this is like scenes from the Holocaust or World War II
admissions you won't find in any history book

but like in concentration camps when stripped to bare essentials.

Like in a novel popular during the '70s
when survivors of a plane crash devoured human flesh.

Or Margaret Garner, the slave who ran away
and murdered her own child rather than to see it become a slave,
in Toni Morrison's novel *Beloved*, she is haunted
by the child's ghost.

Like in Chimamanda Adichie's novel, *Half of a Yellow Sun*
about the Nigerian/Biafra war, a beloved boy character
whom we believed in is so corrupted and dehumanized by war

he participates in a gang rape.
There's a story I heard in South Africa after
the end of apartheid
A boy and his friend rape a girl on the road, they kill her.
The boy eventually turns her over and discovers the girl he raped
and killed was actually his own sister.
A teacher hears this story and screams out to her classroom appalled
asking after all Black people have fought and died for
"Tell me, is this the new South Africa?"
Like that South African boy, Margaret Garner, the subjects of
    Victor Frankl's essays
about the Holocaust and others, some of us in the AIDS crisis
did terrible things to survive.
Never made it down aisles of the hospital wards
of Bellevue and St. Vincent's.
Couldn't bear brown shit-stained walls and
terrible wretched smells of death.
Some of us couldn't bear the hatred and scornful eyes
as we passed the nurses station
saw doctors and family members who blamed us.
Some of us were so grief soaked and waterlogged
we couldn't take one more step
having seen and experienced things in our young lifetimes that
no human being or citizen should.

During Hurricane Katrina, I was in Ghana.
On television, I saw a tidal wave sweep downstairs and trap
a young Black girl.
Firefighters yelled through a basement window
"Hold on, Baby Girl. Just hold on. We're coming. "
But despite hers and their desperate efforts, she drowned.

Some of us were noble, we tried but we just couldn't carry anymore
and were forced to let go
watched bodies devoured,
the very breath and essence stolen
limbs, life support-cut off
some of us went MIA
AWOL
were forced
into black-market drugs and operations like women in the '60s,
using cord, wire hangers, and glass
to abort in back alleys.
Some like Sammy, lover of Michael Brody, father of The Paradise
    Garage,
a beautiful Latino boy with pure soul ravaged by AIDS
shot himself in the head at point blank range
couldn't stand what the virus did to him
the shame he felt
like something out of Kafka's *Metamorphosis*
when a human being is transformed into a bug
we became pariahs, the despised, choosing to wear
in defiance badges, gays in the Holocaust wore pink triangles
like something out of Poe's *The Tell Tale Heart*
Like in *The Diary of Anne Frank*, we hid beneath floorboards
transforming into monsters or messiahs because
as Audre Lorde declared in her battle with cancer
once coming face to face with death, who might ever
have power over us again
Some of us who were witnesses had blinders and
bandages ripped off
developed an x-ray vision
some of us like survivors of the Japanese internment camps

and WWII having lost everything
developed new appreciation for life
For some of us snowfall, rain, water, flowers, a book,
apple, paint brushes, papers, pen took on new meaning
Some of us when we were touched or someone was actually kind
we cried.

The only words I have to describe this time were
The words written by poet Michael Lassell
"How to watch your brother die," and Essex Hemphill's
"When My Brother Fell,"
The only thing that kept us all going were words of Audre,
Essex, Pat Parker, and Joe Beam.
The only thing that freed me from the guilt of
not seeing Don in the hospital was a story I read years
later by bell hooks when she talked about not going
to see a grandmother who was dying, because she said,
"I was the person who loved her most."
When Don died, I was on a hilltop outside of Paris,
like a cord cut
I felt the exact moment breath left his body.
When I returned home from Paris, I saw Max who
was about four years old. We went to a museum together.
The next day I called and Don's surviving lover Steve reported
Max had awakened the day after we went to the museum
and said aloud, after I just begun to believe my friend
Don was dead and gone forever,
"Pamela laughs like Daddy."

Don Reid, Rory Buchanan, Craig Harris, David Frechette, Essex
    Hemphill

are just a few, there are countless others,
So many wakes and funerals I attended paying tribute
to strangers, as if each were a family member of my own
or close friend, but the basis of this story could never be
for thousands, hundreds of thousands who've died,
about massive grief remaining unprocessed, blows endured
to every industry, fashion, literature, business, performance.
It's not about the mysteries, invisible hands, minds, legs,
Behind things I still think, wear, do.
It's not about martyrs who gave and lost lives
so that we now can enjoy freedoms of marriage and
protection under laws.
It's not about men and women I will never forget, faces
publicly streaked with tears, empty caskets carried openly
through streets in protest.
It's not about those like Alan Williams who worked with me
at The Gay and Lesbian Institute, a volunteer who would say
every time I saw him, "You're so beautiful."
He loved to hear the story of how I as a little girl, a little Black girl
would go to the hairdresser as a child and ask the hairdresser
to make my hair whirl and twirl like the figure skater Dorothy Hamill.
"Write that story," he'd say.
This story is not about Tim Boyd, the sign language interpreter
whom I'd often performed with, who died from AIDS
and his mother who still grieves.
It's not about my friend Don Reid, the beautiful collages he made
and the son, lover, and friends he left behind.
It's not about Jody from the South, the first white boy whom I ever
    heard say Y'all
and all those gay boys I met and worked with at a restaurant in Boston,
who disappeared like thousands of bits of paper,

wind just simply took.
Gone, disappeared, like those dissidents of Castro's Cuba
Like the friends and supporters of Allende
this story is not about them
It's not about heroic women, Audre Lorde, June Jordan,
Pat Parker, my grandmother and cancer they fought.
It's not about conspiracies, neglect, nor costumes
I wore.
It's not about today where some people can actually live
with HIV and AIDS.
It's not about those miracle drugs and cocktails, though
I do wish could have gotten here just one day
a moment or second sooner
and saved one more
In the words of Schindler who saved Jews from the Gestapo
and bought their freedom.
Even after he spent his lifetime fortune, he wants to save more.
At the end of the film, he's broken and cries out as if bargaining
with God. "One more. Please God, Just one more."
In my own words after every semester teaching students
seeing so many grow and change but wishing my hands and reach
were big enough and I could save
just one more.
Like Harriet Tubman after every mission, having rescued
over 300 slaves, but said, "if they only knew they were slaves
I could have saved so many more."

No this story is not about them, but like a song is sung
with all of my soul and blood and is dedicated to one person,
one memorial, one funeral, tribute,
where I did not speak.

In this lifetime
there are people with whom you become friends
for reasons unknown
to whom like stars you gravitate
no need for words, long explanation, like a lost or missing piece
of an enormous puzzle,
they just fit,
like when flipping through photographs in an old album,
resemble someone you met once, can't name
but are part of your tribe, a long lost family member
as once described in a book and subsequent film by Alex Haley,
Roots, an autobiography in which he, the grandson
of Southern slaves traces his family tree from Southern plantations
    back to Africa.
The search consumes almost his entire adult life.
Finally, he stumbles upon an African village
containing members, descendants, aunts, uncles, cousins,
grandchildren, and great great grandchildren of his long lost family.
In the film's most memorable and moving sequence, all the
    members of his tribe
and village line up on the edge of a river bank
to greet him. Alex spots them at first by boat.
As if closing a great divide, chasm and loneliness that's existed
in his soul for so long,
he touches the ground and screams out,
"I found you. I've finally found you."
With arms outstretched he and his family embrace,
welcoming and treasuring each other immediately.

This family is who poet Donald Woods was to me.

We met in 1987 outside of a lesbian and gay bookstore
on Hudson Street in the West Village. It was called A Different Light.
Via the grapevine, I heard the literary troupe, Other Countries
was performing and Donald Woods, a star student of Audre Lorde's
was the main attraction.
After the reading's summation, I stood outside on the sidewalk
and met Donald.
No matter how skilled and eloquent his words were,
I was struck by beauty, his elegant and
dark chestnut skin, gleaming teeth, proud mane of dreadlocks
and long lanky stature resembling the African Masai.
Like Alex Haley, I too have endured a lifelong search,
being adopted, I do not know my own history.
I have never known a biological family or experienced physical
    likeness.
So, I imagined in a small but narcissistic way
if my birth parents had had a son, in this lifetime or another
Donald was part of my family, a lost connection, link, or as they say
the missing piece.

In our first conversation outside of A Different Light,
I mentioned offhandedly, "I'm looking for place to stay, Do you
    know any?"
"No," he said thoughtfully. My apartment's tiny. My sister stays
    with me,"
but then added in the generous spirit I came to know,
"You're welcome if you want to sleep on my couch."
I guess I was again struck by Donald and the fact that in 1987
I'd been befriended by a complete stranger who offered me a place
    to sleep.
I didn't accept, but it began a friendship and camaraderie

heightened by frequent dinners, telephone conversations, and
subsequent artistic collaborations.
The most memorable collaboration was at the tribute to Pat Parker,
The pioneering Black lesbian poet who hailed from San Francisco
like Audre Lorde had died prematurely from cancer.
It was an all-star event where Craig Harris and Essex Hemphill
    appeared.
Cheryl Clarke read Pat's signature work,
"Where will you be when they come?"
Donald and I read Pat's work about childrearing
With her signature humor
"Some people think we wake up
chanting to our children
you're gonna be a dyke, you're gonna be a dyke."

In addition to activism and poetry, Donald was part
of a musical group that sang acappella spirituals.
His favorite was an old soul classic titled, "Grandma's Hands."
Seeing him as he sang this song in concert, caused me to write
after his death:
I know if there's heaven,
He's wearing kente cloth
head back
eyes to sky
singing about grandma's hands.

He was pivotal to my development as a poet.
He sometimes grabbed me after a reading like a protective older
    brother,
wrapped his arms around me and said, "God bless this woman,
    bless her."

A few years later, when he disclosed he was HIV positive,
Within months had full blown AIDS, we grew closer
Spent long hours on the telephone talking
when we both should have been at work.

Our most memorable dialogue came during the LA riots
after the Rodney King verdict when white policemen
were acquitted of savagely beating Black motorist Rodney King.
In response, in certain LA neighborhoods Blacks began looting
stores and stealing among many things washing machines.
Donald, as a devout Christian and moral human being
was appalled by the idea of Black people looting stores and stealing
    washing machines
which in my mind aren't in any way restitution for more than
400 years of slavery
equitable recompense for the physical and psychological stress
not a compensatory package for our massive and
remaining scars
So I as a self-styled revolutionary I believed in a
temporary settlement,
while Donald as if he could see all of the gains of our ancestors
    disintegrate,
repeated in shock and disbelief, "Washing machines?!
I can't believe they've stolen washing machines."

In subsequent conversations, his positions on life,
and body weakened.
He left work.
What I didn't know then but know now as
the last time I would ever see him in the flesh
is after I had gone to see him accept an award for his

extraordinary work as the director of AIDS films.
For the honor, he wore a dark blue suit. He resembled a soldier,
a statuesque and decorated warrior recently returned
from fields of World War II.
Donald was proud and only indicated illness after the ceremony
when alone with him.
He asked for a drink of water and held onto my arm feebly
like a young man who'd aged in rapid, meteoric amounts of time.
Weeks later he was emaciated, smothered with KS lesions,
    pneumonia, and bedridden.
He lost motor skills, even ability to control his bowels.

Like many in the end, he did not allow visitors,
needed a nurse to clothe and bathe him.
In our final conversation, he could no longer speak,
but when told by a friend and nurse I was on the line
he whispered into the mouthpiece a barely audible,
"I love you."

I was standing outside of my job at the agency for lesbian
and gay youth when I received news of Donald's passing.
Like a cords of a broken exposed telephone, all I felt were wiry
    fingers
of cold, steel, stock.
As I looked around at the surrounding birds, trees, sky,
all that seemed to remain on that early summer day only the ground
looked welcoming like a cool and restful mat, I wanted to lie down on,
press my ears, face against it to feel closer to Donald.
I wanted to lay down, rolling back and forth,
screaming out, the way I'd seen one grief stricken young man
do on the late spring day Rory Buchanan died.

He laid on the pavement outside of the funeral home and
screamed rocking and rolling the way people in some Black
    Pentecostal
churches do when someone's possessed by spirits
or the holy ghost
Or at funerals when grief gets too much
The way I'd seen once at a childhood family cookout
too much lighter fluid caused a gas grill to blow up
my father shielded me but I suffered third degree burns.
My aunt's clothes caught fire, she tried to put it out by laying down
on the ground and rolled back and forth to relieve the horror
and sensation of skin and flesh burning.
The same way I'd seen my father do when his mother, my beloved
    grandmother
died, he picked up her face and from the casket and kissed her.
My grandfather's skin too was on fire and he shouted, I will meet
    you, Pearl,
at those pearly gates
Wanting to join his partner in heaven.

This was all I felt, every emotion held, while I sat at the memorial
for Donald where I was not asked and did not speak.
The memorial had been arranged by Other Countries, and his
    brothers
had full control.
Perhaps they too were weary, tired of the Funeral Diva.
Perhaps they wanted a new person, a fresher face,
but to see and hear all of them assembled who at that moment
seemed to be strangers, it was all I could do to show restraint,
not scream out at the top of my lungs—
None of you really knew him as I did, he was my brother.

For a politico, a so-called revolutionary, someone belonging
to a larger picture, these were selfish thoughts, but I needed in one
    way
to clear the room, be alone with Donald once more,
like during our intimate phone talks, to place my ear against his,
treasure our bond, but in another way,
I had simply wanted to speak.

At the funeral, inside of the church loyalties again were divided
between some of Donald's activist lesbian and gay family
and his biological one.
Like him Donald's immediate family was devoutly Christian
at odds with the fact he was gay and purposefully failed to mention
in the program or eulogy one thing most important
Donald lived most of thirty-three years as an out gay man
Like Rory Buchanan, Craig Harris, Alan Williams,
Don Reid, David Frechette, he died of AIDS. Like our elders
Audre Lorde, Pat Parker, and James Baldwin he was a
pioneering figure in a Black lesbian and gay literary movement.
All of them died with dignity, fighting for rights of lesbian and gay
    people.
They did not die in shame.
This glaring omission ignited our fury and caused
the late great activist and poet Assotto Saint, a brown-skinned man
whose own recent AIDS diagnosis was a ticking time bomb
who stood more than 6' 5" in stocking feet, a self-proclaimed diva
with a French Haitian accent used for effect,
to rise from his pew, saunter down the church's long aisle like a
    Parisian
model walking on a runway with determination

speed and attitude, he stormed the pulpit, uninvited
slammed his hand on the bible as done when one wants
to tell truth
to everyone's shock he screamed, "Donald Woods was a
proud Black gay man, he did not die of heart failure.
He died of AIDS. If you agree with me, stand up."
As in the way I met Donald without questioning I leapt
to my feet and felt for the first time in a ceremony of
pomp and circumstance—free.
In my peripheral vision I saw a room full of strangers
divided by politics and identity
In the middle stood Donald's biological sister.
For all of the stated reasons, I felt a strange affinity with her
like between us was an unspoken bond
like distant stars always having shared the same love
from a different proximity.

EPILOGUE:

Twenty years later I received a call from Gregg Bordowitz who asked
me to read poetry at a tribute to Other Countries at the Whitney Museum.
Without knowing our relationship, he asked me to speak about Donald Woods.
"He was one of my best friends," I said.
At the tribute, I read David Frechette's poem, "Je Ne Regrette Rien"
as well as Essex Hemphill's, "When My Brother Fell."
I also read Donald Woods's poem, "Prescription."
I read an inscription Donald had written to me
on the inside cover of Brother to Brother, *a Black gay male anthology:*
Dear Pamela,
Thank you for appreciating the love of brothers for brothers.

Love is the light of the world.
When I finished there wasn't a dry eye.
Later in an unfinished poem I would describe that moment
As I imagined a soldier would,
"I had to go back to the warfront, to reconstruct his body parts,
and bring him home."
And I felt like Alex Haley finally closing a chasm,
a great divide in his soul
having put my brother to proper rest.

There are many things to update, since Rodney King,
at this time the number of police killings has increased against Black men
and reached crisis proportions.
I do not believe as some writers do that this violence is new, only
the cameras are. America is imploding
from crimes of the past.
Those of us who are left from that Black lesbian and gay literary
scene still write.
After a period of silence
we are finally able to process
and writing about that time has begun to flourish.
Documenting the lives of Black lesbians and gays who died
of AIDS and cancer is part of my life's work.
I am a professor.
I feel often like the daughter of Kizzy in Roots who returns
to the grave of her father the famous runaway
Kunta Kinte.
In defiance, she scratches off his slave name Toby on a wooden marker
and writes his preferred and biological name Kunta Kinte

as if to say as I am saying now, we are still here.

Don's son Baby Max is a young man like his father

He has become a visual artist.

He still struggles with the loss of his fathers to AIDS.

There is a picture of Donald and me at a gay pride event in March 1991.

He is holding my waist and we are looking out and smiling.

At present, I am in love. One day at a time.

Some days I look at her and wish like Alex Haley after a lifelong search,

I could shout "I found you. Finally, I found you."

This piece took fifteen years to write.

I am tired.

I can feel the hands of Donald, Don Reid, David Frechette,

Rory Buchanan, Bert Hunter, Alan Williams, Audre Lorde,

Pat Parker, Marlon Riggs, Essex Hemphill, and Assotto Saint pushing me

across the finish line.

NEVER AGAIN

At the end of every Holocaust film I've seen and
there are not many
they show real life survivors and say the words
Never Again
Some of us like me/stare into these films
down the long tunnels of history wondering
how it could have ever happened at all
that a leader and his minions could be so toxic, poisonous
you'd turn against your neighbors
you could be so oblivious, brainwashed, scared
desperate to be superior or to survive
you'd do anything, or almost.
They say never again
but it is again
as I look at the deportations
round-ups
I'm reminded of Idi Amin when he cast out foreigners
and Forest Whitaker in the film *The Last King of Scotland*, when he
    played him.
And to see it is again
at rallies, at protests, they show the coat hangers and crude
    instruments

women were forced to use in back alley abortions
We say never again but taking away women's choice
and Planned Parenthood, it is again.
Today started out in an argument with someone
who didn't understand why I mentioned race so much
in my new book
and that white man is not the first/a Black woman
asked too.
I wanted to scream HELLO haven't you seen the news
Didn't you see what happened to Stephon Clark
unarmed and shot in the back six times by police
And who even cares what happens to women
Black lesbians, lesbians of color
There's no public outcry.
A student once wrote to me in an academic paper
that a parent forced her to stop playing sports
because they said sports made her more of a dyke
It killed my student inside because she was an athlete
So the white guy I argued with about my book
said he was just giving me some good advice
from his experience as an empath
I said I don't need your advice
I have reasons for talking about race and gender in the
    interpersonal
He said he was just trying to help me.
I'll offer this nonsequitur
Winnie Mandela died a few years ago
She had great impact on me
I read she was nobility
But then the difference between her and how Princess Diana was
    treated

Everyone accepted and loved Diana's silent/passive status
She was allowed to be gorgeous
No one ever associated her with that colonial stain
There are moments in the recent Winnie Mandela documentary
that stand out to me
where she buried her face in her hands and screamed out
I've been betrayed
the other moment was when she said she was
the only ANC member brought to TRC
and made to testify
Nelson Mandela forgave a nation
but he could never forgive her.
What was done to Winnie is done to other Black women
and working artists
Black women fighting to give language/resistance
but it only matters when a celebrity says or does it.
At Cape Coast Castle in Ghana after you've passed
The Door of No Return
there is a plaque donated to the Castle by Black tribal elders
It reads:
May we never sell ourselves into slavery again
But it is Again.

UNTITLED

Say what you want about my mother/ I know
her cruelty knew no bounds
neglect
never a warm hug
kind word
every year when school came/fall
I looked at the flyers of back-to-school clothes
Nothing
I wore rags/hand-me-downs
As soon as I worked she made me pay rent
and that was the message engraved into me
instead of being taught responsibility
I was taught I owed
her rent
the ground I stood on and had no rights
My father's neglect
The patches put over his eyes
not to see
never a book
nothing
She suffered from mental illness
was selfish
Through blinds

Through stories I get glimpses
Say what you want but she is the greatest fighter
She is going now
She cobbles out a life from the women she watches on housewives
    shows
Their competition
Her neighbor buys a wreath
My mother buys a bigger one
She tells my father when I visit
Strike up the barbeque
She buys corn
pretends it's a party
I see she has lost weight this visit
the depression she believes there is a man coming
to destroy things
and there are bugs
She constantly buys poison
I know I can't talk to her about depression/the drugs
So I say as gently as I can
Keep your spirits up/ then you will gain back the weight
On the morning I am leaving
She dresses up in nice clothes
And a pair of coral earrings I gave her
She said she'd been skipping meals
But on the morning before I left
perhaps just as a child to show me
She piled her plate full of scrambled eggs with ketchup
and she ate.

RUTH VICK

I was reticent about posting about my
first mother's death on FB
We weren't close
and you know the attention-seeking
nature of it all
But then I felt less bad
when somebody posted about their
missing pet
The condolences concerns
were far reaching
And then I thought another Black woman
died today in agony
Poor Black and alone
My aunt said the wake was pathetic
There was no one there
Said she left after 5 or 10 minutes
Her brother's first wife
My adoptive mom
My father called me to say she was
Being buried an hour before I went on stage
He needed someone to talk to
I think they said she was cremated
I was surprised I felt as much as I did

Given her life-long absence
I know now in retrospect she was fleeing
for her life
from abuse
She tried to take me
but that failed
If you see your father, she said
Don't go near him
But I was four and must have
missed him so bad
When I saw the car I screamed Daddy
and ran to him
Get in, he said
and we drove away after he'd
chased her into the house
And said I'm taking her/I'm
taking your daughter away.

My father remarried
and his new wife forbade me
from seeing her
I was six
I know though she was sick with many
things for a long time
I know she adopted another daughter
to replace me
But I know I was part of my first mother's agony
on her death bed
I know I was that pain aching her bones
Her stomach her head
I was that baby ghost

I was that beloved
I know somewhere she blamed herself
It's always the woman's fault
My father was a monster I know
But he was the parent I knew
I didn't ask for condolences on FB
I asked people instead to say her name
Ruth Vick.

THERE IS ME/THERE IS MY MOTHER

It is courageous/
I am doing that thing now my mother/stepmother could not do.
She tried.
She practiced.
I will never forget the blue suitcase/ a square that looked
almost like an attaché case/only larger
It was always the same song and dance routine
whenever she fought with my father
She'd pull the blue suitcase out of her closet
She'd pack the case
Leaving it to sit by the door
She'd scream to my father, I'm leaving you
and then the bullet
I'm also taking your daughter
You're coming with me right?
I really had no choice
I knew she wouldn't leave
and I'd be stuck with her wrath
I wanted her to go
I wanted to stay with my father but I couldn't say that
My mother tried but never made it further than the stairwell
Maybe once she made it down the stairs and
he dragged her back

Call the police, she commanded to my six-year-old self
Maybe once or twice she made it down to the parking lot
and into their car/the emerald green Impala
Maybe he clung to the side of the car door and threatened
As Toni Morrison once described in *Beloved*
Besides the main character Sethe
There was a girl so traumatized by her sister's ghost
A baby whose throat was slit by her mother
She could never get past the yard
I imagine how many slaves tried/as opposed to got away
How many made it down to the garden or potato patch
With thoughts and sights on freedom but turned back for fear/
How many as I have got trapped, could never get their foot loose.
My mother practiced but could never escape.
I see the end results/a depression that can't be overcome.
Mental illness left untreated
That eats away her brain.
She believes there are bugs
and a man who comes to the house and steals from her
She buys poison and puts it down daily
The worst part is that through abuse she's been made into
a man's raggedy doll
So I am doing now what my mother could not do
Though it's late
Though I should have done it long ago
Moving away from abuse
Emptying
Going back to the beginning
It's frightening to start over
Reshape my own core
What I do have

What my mother and I share is an
Indomitable spirit
Just when you think it's impossible/an obstacle can't be overcome
There is me/there is my mother
As in a medical drama when you think the patient
has lost too much blood
Suffered too many wounds
There is me/there is my mother
It's like an action drama
Where the hero fleeing a villain
Clings for life from a rooftop
Awaiting rescue/ there is me/there is my mother.

MYSTI

My mother's cat Mysti
Spelled M Y S T I
Doesn't just walk/she strides
black cat/healthy fur/shiny coat looks like bat girl
It isn't incidental, she is Black, a girl
The great survivor in my parent's lineage of pets
She although six years old never stops playing and is my mother's
constant sidekick
like me once but an involuntary one in card games and watching TV
yes this cat strides confident
has never known war or brutality
can't and doesn't ingest as humans do the daily injustices
another unarmed Black boy shot twenty times by police
Mysti doesn't know the violation of girls
Hasn't had her fur touched in peculiar ways
In fact I was surprised my parents picked her
Given their insanity, racism, and superstition
But she has brought my family so much joy and for that
I love her
Love that she tilts her head at times when you talk as if she's trying
    to listen
And comprehend
Sometimes when I visit my father will say to her, "Get in your bed"

And she lays down on a soft spot in my luggage
That she finds a piece of red yarn and drops it at my feet
Inviting me to play
Something I thought only dogs did
That when you are alone and pondering she reaches her paw out
To let you know she is there
That she lays beside me quietly when I make collages
And when I finish she sits squarely in the middle
Once when I was leaving
She was upset and she raced up and down a hallway
From my room to the room where the front door is
And I saw her tiny bat ears peeking above the step
She is my mother's warrior against all
The pawn that she threatens my father with
If I leave I'm taking my cat
She knows that's the dagger
I suppose the battle in old age is loneliness
She and the cat miss me
My mother, an artist, has started doing large scale puzzles.
They always worked in the basement of the house
When I call my mother says, "Guess what?"
"Me and Mysti are now doing puzzles in your room"
I start to laugh
I thought about visual artists, how they use the phrase
Activating the space
I imagine Mysti and my mother activating the space
of my family bedroom
Keeping me there in spirit
Bringing me home.

SIDEWALK RAGE

I'm not sure why but it's taken forever for me to write this poem
I hope to remember all the pieces
But I've developed a new condition
One that's come from age/I can no longer take the shit I once did
And there's a part of my condition that comes from gentrification
And cell phone use
Living amidst tech zombies
And their general fear and hatred of POC
My condition is called sidewalk rage
Kind of like road rage
But comes when walking down the street and there's some millennial
Who has just moved into the neighborhood
who thinks it's theirs
a white girl who in broad daylight feels a dark presence
walking behind her
It's me/minding my own business and she gets so panicked and
    paralyzed
she stops walking and holds her purse
with my new condition I yell
If you don't want to live around Black people get the fuck out of
    the neighborhood!
She is shocked.
Or in another scenario
You see random white women on their phones

Standing in a doorway completely blocking it
Because you know only they exist
And you're like HELLO, HELLO
Yes, all these years I thought I was still a small town girl and then
  suddenly
with my sidewalk rage, I'm a bonafide New Yorker
like the ones you've seen on bicycles banging on the hood
of a taxi cab that tries to cut them off
My person with sidewalk rage is a character of their own
Where once I was silent
Recently I confronted a man who was blocking my path/crossing
  the street
He had his head down and almost rammed into me
I sucked my teeth loud and shouted HELLO, HELLO, MOVE
He was so angry I'd confronted him, he yelled, Suck my dick
I started to yell something profane but I stopped myself
And then I was in the subway/going downstairs and a white man
  rammed into me
On the phone
My sidewalk rage kicked in and thought for a second to sneak behind him
And kick him down the stairs
That's my sidewalk rage/ I stopped myself.
I don't know who this person is in me who would never speak up
  for herself
Was always soft and vulnerable
Who's been at various times pickpocketed, blasphemed,
body-slammed, ransacked, ridiculed
Who now has a voice
Who now lets rage show
Who couldn't express herself
Has now become all angles and sharp edges.

YOU CAN'T GET OUT FROM UNDER

I may attach this to another poem and
I may not
This may stand on its own
But these are my jokes
If you happen to go outside and see some lady/some bitch
on the street/50-ish
coat open/it's under 20 degrees
don't yell, Are you fucking crazy?
Leave her alone, she's in menopause.
Zero degrees/hot flash
And that shit feels good
Also, if you're on a bus or a train and you
really need to sit down/find a Black man
A big Black man/next to him
the seat is always empty
Next to big Black women too.
Sometimes on a crowded bus to Boston
The seat next to me is completely empty
And just so you know I'm in a rage about crudité
FUCK crudité
Who eats crudité except for starving first-year college students
at a book party
Really what middle-aged person do you know is gonna chew hard

on a carrot stick at a party
It's not a barn.

You're not a sheep or some shit.

I mean, what about sensitivity to people with fake-ass teeth
I looked over recently at an event and saw some Brussel sprouts
on a platter of crudité at a party
Raw ass/hard ass Brussel sprouts
No one is going to eat raw Brussel sprouts at a party.

To my point, no one touched them.

And politics has ruined my ability to enjoy Christmas or escape.
I love Christmas.

I watched *Frosty the Snowman* with my mother over the holiday
But then politics came in.

I started questioning if the relationship between Frosty
and the little girl who loved him was age-appropriate.

Why did they hug so fucking much?

I know he's supposed to be snow but just why was he so fucking white
Like hundreds of years of patriarchy you can't get out from under.

My new accountant has ton of jokes, he's a Black man
He said the revolution is coming and
To those who say they don't serve Blacks,
it's okay because we don't eat 'em
LOL

Anyway, today, TBH I feel like Patsy in *Twelve Years a Slave*
Beaten for picking cotton.

I mean I like someone who is white.

Their partner is white.

They have stocks, trust funds, and a retirement plan
And I feel like fucking Patsy in *Twelve Years a Slave*
Alternately known as Mammy.

TWIZZLERS

Size color class I was never allowed to be little
by little I mean innocent
by little I mean allowed to play
make mistakes
If anything occurred in whatever setting
I was always blamed
I was mistaken constantly for being older than I was
At six when my stepmother came she refused to
allow me alone time with my father
If a moment occurred she asked
What were you doing with him?
As if I at six were molesting my father
I was caught once through an open bathrobe
trying to see my father's penis
My stepmother never forgot
You were trying to look at him, she said.
I was not given toys books anything
Stuffed animals
Bows ribbons anything that may be attached to a little girl
I was also my mother's sounding board for her adult problems
with my Dad
Constantly instructed to call the police
when he hit her

The only thing my parents could figure out to do together
for some small infraction was to give me punishment
Two weeks
So I never knew the nurturance
that girls got
My adult life has duplicated this
always to blame
always outside
refusing to see my little girl
On occasion my mother sent me to the store to get candy
Things that she liked
Fire balls
Reese's peanut butter cups
Kit Kat bars
Black licorice
Sometimes red which I liked
Twizzlers
I remember once chewing a pack of red Twizzlers as an adult
the red stem hung out of my mouth
A friend at the time exclaimed
You're such a little girl . . .
And once when I was with a woman
Someone looked on and said, Oh
your little girl is out
In relationships too I was never
the little girl
In fact in most of them I rescued radically immature women
I was their mother caretaker
the one with all responsibility
And of course when it ended I was always to blame
Everything to me lies around class race gender lines

Even in so-called evolved communities
Even with POC
I always know no one would treat a white-skinned woman
or a man the way I've been treated
In colleges where I teach
I'm always aware of the hierarchy
People screaming about diversity
I moan complain
How the AIDS narrative only belongs to men
They never ask women
Black women
As if AIDS didn't happen to us
Our fathers brothers sons nephews
cousins acquaintances
The Black gay boys in the choir
became our disappeared
I remember a pair of Black gay men
who were spiritual
would act as ministers
and bury the dead Black boys
families wouldn't recognize
These men showed up as the priests
and gave last rites
And what of the women
A mother nursing a grown son
returned to a baby
ravaged by AIDS
Me being young myself going into sick wards
like leper colonies
seeing those abandoned by society
I never forgot

Even my era did not allow me to be little
innocent
A threat if I spoke up
A competitor for middle class white girls
who had the world handed to them
And resented me/you for surviving
thriving despite all odds.

PARABLE OF THE SOWER

If you want to know the ending
How it's all gonna turn out
The aftermath of Trump's presidency
Don't turn to analysts, Wall Street, or CNN
For an accurate portrait of where it's all going
what it's gonna look like
reread Octavia Butler's *Parable of the Sower*
set in California in 2027
People in fear/behind walls/gated communities
a woman raped so much
she can't stand
gun violence/addiction/fires that can scarcely
be put out
people scavenging for food/trying not to become prey
compassion is gone
the main character named Lauren is a hyper-empath
she can feel others' pain
which I think is a metaphor for artists
whatever you think of Marina Abramovic
her show title is right
The Artist is Present
from the beginning of time until now
Look again at the *Hunger Games*, the districts are

actually concentration camps with gray garb and barbed fences
that nod to Nazi Germany
Humans are pitted against each other to survive
Sometime after Trayvon Martin was shot, I finally understood
something deep about *Star Wars*
I've always rooted for good guys/always
Once I heard a friend at the movies rooting for Poison Ivy/
Batman and Bat Girl's nemesis
I was shocked that anyone could root for a bad girl
But after Trayvon was killed by George Zimmerman
who walked free
I finally understood what could turn a character's eyes dark
You could become so disillusioned
And then I understood in the *Star Wars* franchise
what made Darth Vader—Vader
I felt that again after Trump's election
No more green, blue light
Only gray, dark drab, white bones, war
Last week, I worked with a class I hadn't met before
On the subject of Black Lives Matter
I repeated something Gregg Bordowitz said to a group of students
"What if the only justice we have right now is here in this room?"
One student said, "Nothing ever changes."
So I responded by asking, "Are you telling me then
you can't change?"
They were all surprised, shocked by my question.
At the end, I asked the class, "What have you learned today?"
A Black girl answered as if she were channeling Octavia herself,
"Change,
is up to us."

PARABLE OF THE SOWER 2

Parable of the Sower by Octavia Butler is a dystopian science
   fiction novel
set in Los Angeles 2027
the protagonist is a sixteen-year-old Black girl named Lauren Olmeeda.
She is a hyper-empath who amongst war, hunger, gun violence,
   rape, and addiction,
builds a new faith called Earthseed where she reinvents God,
says God is change.
I've taught this book for many semesters at college
I think it's profound and prophetic and the students, mainly
   students of color
aren't used to Black girl protagonists.
I ask my students how they feel about a Black girl protagonist
who creates and practices her own religion,
which I think is sheer genius.
I ask, "Is anyone allowed to create their own religion, why or why not?"
The students are always puzzled by these questions as it's nothing they
are used to.
Somehow, in all of my readings and discussions of this work,
I missed something obvious about a Black girl building her own religion
amidst war, isolation, and gun violence.
Although, I did understand that Octavia Butler was forewarning us
   about

issues that would plague us in a not so far away future.
Also, in the novel she warns of a water crisis and in one of her
books she warns of a character/a politician who would come to
  power
with the rhetoric of "Make America Great Again"
she wrote this over twenty years ago.
She not only warned us but in the same seed/breath
gave an answer
Told us in the midst of chaos and destruction, to create something new.
"God," she said through Lauren Olmeeda, "is change."

Since the election and this new year I've been mulling over this epiphany
as I contemplate change in my own life asking myself
what am I willing to do differently
I'm tired of the schizophrenia of activism, two lives
living separate and opposite
people who say Black Lives Matter but secretly or openly attack
  Black women
and Black women and Women of Color are the biggest perpetrators
  of this
Then there are those who say they love queers, but are ashamed/
value straights/anyone over other queers.
Trans peoples lives are not the only lives at stake here.
I have never been safe.
I got a text recently after the New Year from a former student
of mine.
She is a Black lesbian. She invited me to a show.
I had worked with and helped her.
In an act of what I can only guess was self-hatred, as I once watched her
adore white men regardless of what they gave,
she and another Black woman led students in an elite school

to attack me.

It was brutal and I won't recall the gory details.

For the most part, until now, I've stayed publicly silent,

but the results and repercussions in my life were long-lasting.

I was so stressed after the event occurred, a few years ago,

I fell down in my apartment and needed six stitches over my eye.

I never had stitches before.

I fell on a sharp plastic object that just missed my eyeball.

For her fear, hatred, and slander, I could have lost my eyesight.

Even the doctor who stitched me up said

"You'll never get rid of the scar, it will last a lifetime,"

and it has.

I saw another woman/an ex-lover this past New Year's day.

She's a poet.

I saw her at an event and she was smiling at me.

Twenty years later, you could see she'd forgiven herself.

She looked so happy and at peace.

Everybody I believe should be happy and let go,

but I couldn't go and say to her

like the scar over my eye, the wounds from our relationship

were long-lasting/ that for years she and all of her friends

all white women who I don't even know/harassed me

and spread wild rumors and gossip

because I am a tall Black dark lesbian from the working class

they all assumed like Susan Smith, a white woman who accused a

random Black man of killing her kids when she herself was culpable

They all said I did it.

For years I grieved, lost weight, and more.

One of the games some former friends played is they'd

invite me to parties

then pretend they couldn't see me,

though I was the tallest, darkest there.

I will never forget one of my ex-lover's exes who used to try to sleep
with me, helped my ex in a vicious campaign,
sat a dinner table with me just recently and pretended we'd never met.
She stuck her hand out and said, "Hi, I'm . . . "
I said, "I know who you are," and laughed.
Actually, I was in shock.
I was in a museum the other day seeing the work of Kerry James
    Marshall
and I passed by Ralph Ellison's classic, *The Invisible Man*
There was an article going around the internet about high schools
and they said the most discriminated against,
the persons falling through the cracks, the most unseen,
most unlikely to have needs met,
most likely sent to detention were Black girls.
I know I'm not a girl/I'm a woman
A friend of mine recently
told me to grow up/stand up/fight for myself/she's right
but there are repercussions for me as a Black woman making myself
visible that she could never know
that my entire upbringing and society silences me
I'll put my friend's comments in the category of
another white woman with a trust fund/has never been to therapy
rarely has had a job/takes recreational pictures all day and told
me once flippantly, "You should work harder."
I won't say how old I am but at this age
I feel like Benazir Bhutto emerging from exile
I've been thinking about taking art classes and driving lessons
Things I've never done
And I feel like Dorothy Allison said about when she chose to write
I am just beginning to live.

BEY

I have to say I envy Beyoncé
That she gets to show up after the fact in New Orleans
With her hair and make-up did
Going down on a police car
That she epitomizes Black cool
With a voice-over from Messy Mya and Big Freedia
The Queen of sissy bounce
I envy her Lemonade when she got to have Serena twerking
A few frames before the mothers of sons lost to police violence
And no one called her out on that
I envy her Black Panther and feminist garb in Formation
That she is a declared feminist
It's like being the first wife or something
The one who bore the kids
Whose body got stretched out
Didn't care for herself
Got tired and too caught up
Disillusioned
Had needs
The one who got left for a glamorous other
Because real life activism isn't that glam
There's lots of loss and invisibility
And it's just incredulous you hear people saying things like

She's so beautiful
Admiring her hair and make-up
And will pay anything to hear her sing
And relish in the Bey and Jay soap opera
Talk about how abused she is
While there are still so many real-life Black women
Standing right next to you
Who are also beautiful
Whose lives got used up paving the way
And you wouldn't pay ten dollars or a dime to hear
The people of New Orleans are still struggling
Lost their homes
Their city
I always teach the work of Safiya Bukhari, a Black Panther
Who died in prison at fifty-three years old
Advocating for the rights of political prisoners
It's a simple book
It always calls out to me.

UPRISING

Sixteen years old
from the suburbs, Boston
I'd go into the city shopping
with my cousin and friends
we'd venture into Boston Commons, the Park.
There were hustlers there, I didn't know then
with a set-up table.
They played some sort of game with shells
hid money under a shell or a plastic cup
moved their hands real quick
made it purposefully look so easy
naïve sixteen years old, I bet
fifty dollars, a lot of money for me then.
They made it look so easy.
You just had to pick the right one.
Of course, it was rigged
I lost
felt dizzy,
sick to my stomach
lost my gaze.
On Tuesday night after the election I felt the same way
heisted in a shell game.
Walking outside on Wednesday, in my neighborhood

a white woman who barely ever speaks was crying
asked, "What do we do?"
I answered earnestly, a teacher, an artist, professor
who always tries, "I don't know."
Later, I walked up the street, a white man in an SUV
with the window down drove by.
He wore an expensive business suit
had a big brown cigar
like when babies are born
expensive like in gangsta films
like *Goodfellas*
or on
The Sopranos after a kill.
He looked happy, smug,
that's when I realized the Trump Presidency is a hustler's game
Ballers club
Players only
Pimp paradise
Wives with teased hair and lots of plastic surgery
on the white BET.
They made it all look so easy
like a choice
Who knew
The American Dream was a side hustle for big businessmen
with all their ugly red white blue striped flag merchandising
available at Walmart and Target, I'll never buy into again
Who knew
Freedom was a marketing idea/consumer product
Hallucinatory drug cooked up in some Rove-ian as in Karl type of
laboratory sweatshop
Maintained by the architects of apartheid
Freedom like air if you're white and male and rich enough

to keep breathing
Today, I started to cry as I wrote
to my students
knowing that in everything so far, I've tried to protect them
and realizing there are places in this world
even my maternal hands can't reach.
In Poland, the Warsaw ghetto against a Nazi fascist regime
On Southern Plantations, in fields, in Haiti
On shores of Africa
Uprising
The '60s
The streets
James
Nina
Bayard
Miriam
June
Nikki
Lorraine
Audre
Pat
Malcom
Martin
Betty
Sekou
The Unnamed
Artists
Poets
Teachers
Always
Uprising.

POST-ELECTION

Like trinkets sold at gift shops
near former slave sites
masks carved for tourist consumption
paper promises given to those getting off the boat
from somewhere
those who crossed the desert, dehydrated
raped, throat slit, still
arrived by foot
Like dollar-off coupons at Target
going fast/buy now
Hope and democracy are a poor woman's
last pennies spent to buy Christmas lights
and ribbon at Rite-Aid
Like children's drawings with multicolored crayons
displayed in elementary school windows
Are what mothers fight for when their child
is killed in a school shootout by an imbecile
who had easy access to guns
All the shooter wanted was to be like Kanye, a star.
Like Dylan Roof in a courtroom shouting, "It's not fair,"
hearing the family of victims testify
after he shot nine Black parishioners while their heads
were bowed and they were praying

The cops after took him to Burger King
Like Jeffery Dahmer who ate the flesh and hearts
of young Black boys
He was killed in prison/stuffed in a broom closet
And like the leader of the Rwandan massacre
like a poet once said of an abusive father
I'm glad
So glad
he's dead
Like candy spun by politicians
dissolving as soon as your tongue reaches to taste it
Hope and democracy are just words
evading Walter Scott
Trayvon Martin
Emmett Till
Mike Brown
Akai Gurley
Gift and Sandra Bland
Hope and democracy are like old Harlequin romance novels/extinct
As my friend says, "There's no more love,
only drama"
Hope and democracy are slogans
written on cups in souvenir shops on 42nd Street
having nothing to do with our lives
reality.

ROPE-A-DOPE

FOR SANDRA BLAND

I had just begun to relax
celebrate the marriage equality ruling
I had just begun feeling with Obama I was
watching Ali in trouble off the ropes
delivering to his opponents the rope-a-dope
my father's eyes
excitement
I was just beginning to breathe air
feel exhilarated at images of Joe Biden
and President Obama running
down halls of the White House with rainbow flags
like boys with kites-soaring
I was just beginning to forgive deaths of my brothers
to AIDS
not forget
there should still be tribunals
for them and every woman abused
by the medical system
I had just begun to turn a corner on Mike Brown, Freddie Gray
Trayvon Martin, Eric Garner, the massacre at AME
not think of it all everyday

Then the police kill this young Black girl in custody in Texas
claim she committed suicide
I remember we're a war nation
in war times
I imagine how James, Bayard, Nina felt
seeing a nation turn its dogs, teeth, gas, hoses, bullets,
on children, adults, humans
I can't stop thinking about Steve Biko
his battered face
they say he hung himself too
the world's outrage
who will pray now
for us
America.

SILENCE=DEATH

Speaking to my former student at SAIC, a writer and visual artist
They say there's not one day that passes when at some point
They don't return to the first reading I gave to the class
on Audre Lorde
The Transformation of Silence into Language and Action and
Poetry is not a Luxury
In a final paper, another student said she was floored
but in the end grateful for the Audre Lorde checklist I handed out
at the start of class
Asking what are the words you do not yet have?
What do you need to say
What are the tyrannies you swallow day by day
and attempt to make your own until you will sicken and die from
    them,
Still in silence
List them and write a new list tomorrow and the day after
This in mind when I think about the image and words
Silence=Death
Like my students I return to the master teacher Black lesbian warrior
mother cancer survivor and poet Audre Lorde
I return also to the essay "The Transformation of Silence into
    Language and Action"
with the instructions for living

Silence will not protect you
In this great dragon called America
that attempts to wipe us out
and it's machinery that attempts to grind us
into dust
It is better to speak knowing we were never meant to survive
So yesterday when I saw that poster silence equals death in the
    windows
of the Leslie Lohman Museum
That pink triangle on black paper
from blocks away
It called to me like a beacon
Amidst societal madness/personal struggles and the Trump
    presidency
to never give up
It reminded me too of a generation of gay and lesbian warriors who
    are no longer here with us
felled to AIDS and cancer
But on their deathbeds used the mantra to inspire
Silence=Death
I think about when Black gay and Latinx poets Essex Hemphill
Donald Woods
Don Reid
Roy Gonsalves
Rory Buchanan
David Frechette
Craig Harris
Alan Williams and Assotto Saint and so many more were still here
How their black hair began to sprout twists and knots go wild and
    kinky
to signify early Black gay consciousness

I think about when I first met Donald Woods outside of a
   bookstore
in the West Village called A Different Light and we fell in love
We were all so young Black awkward and gangly but fierce and
   determined.

Donald was Audre Lorde's student at Hunter
For all of us Black gay and lesbians struggling to find our way
Lorde was our guru
I think about poetry readings that happened all the time at
the Community Center on 13th Street
We were upstairs while ACT UP met downstairs
There were Black gay and bisexual poets Storme Webber
Cheryl Clarke
Jewelle Gomez
Sapphire
As Black gay people we couldn't afford to get arrested so we wrote
performed and sang revolution
Like the salons of the Harlem Renaissance
featuring Zora's Neal Hurston and Langston Hughes
These meetings informed me forever
I also saw plague and cancer decimate my people
People I imagined growing old with artists who knew at that time
they only had moments and seconds to live so they wrote
It was right after his diagnosis I saw Assotto Saint
performing on top of the tables at The Gay and Lesbian
   Community Center
I will never forget when he stormed the pulpit at Donald Woods'
   funeral
I learned what it was like to make work with urgency as Audre said
as though your life depended upon it

to know you couldn't waste a moment or a second
I learned more about being an artist in the early '90s than any
  college education
ever taught me
It was from little boys with baby faces and death sentences who
  spoke
and forced themselves into the world at all odds I learned
From little and big boys and girls in the face of catastrophe
Raising their fists as Avram did last night
Uttering the mantra
Silence=Death.

FOR DONALD WOODS

On the warm spring day Rory Buchanan died his friend
a beautiful young Black gay man lay down on the ground
outside of the funeral home and let out a gut wrenching scream
He lay down on the ground, rolled back and forth as he cried.
He did what we all felt but didn't have the courage to do
expressed in his actions battle fatigue, weariness
of a young community that had lost so many of its own
This might have been one month before we lost poet Donald
    Woods
and members of a Black lesbian and gay community poured into a
    packed church
hot humid with no outlet
Poet Assotto Saint stood more than 6' 5" in heels, but on that day
he wore a man's suit and performed an act of exorcism and protest
when he assailed the pulpit took over said Donald Woods did not
    die
of heart failure, he died of AIDS and he was a proud Black gay man
If you agree with me stand up
And so today Whitney Houston is gone, Etta James, my idol,
the soul train man who shot himself Don Cornelius, Heavy D,
    Howard Tate, Michael Jackson, Prince, Muhammad Ali
Heath Ledger, Anna Nicole, Amy Winehouse
Nelson Mandela

so many who helped us know who we are and were
but today I don't want any lavish displays of grief and protest
to do as they did in the Black church when spirit took hold
you could see a weighted 300-pound body fly up and dance
Today I want none of what happened with Rory or Donald
Today I want to breathe breath let go past pain grief
be the girl I was leap up sing dance not care
let my tongue turn blue eating an icy
walk down the street carrying a boom box
singing Stephanie Mills, "I Feel Good All Over"
to feel like I do when snow falls taking that first big gulp
of something new
the way I feel every time I board the plane to Africa or Europe
and I'm racing over images stalls upon stalls
filled with beauty and mystery
to feel with myself the way students express feeling with me
eyes open it affects everything
to feel the way I do walking up the hill to a new school
like a traveling preacher filled up with message
Today I want to release all the things I could
should have said
be the student who said I changed everything
even at home
my teachings made him grow up
become a new and better man.

HOLD TIGHT

On the Orlando shooting:
Let's be clear, it wasn't Isis or Islam
that licensed that man to walk into a gay bar
and massacre those white and gay POC
It was America with heinous gun laws that allow any white
or white-skinned man with mental health problems
to purchase weapons of war/machine guns with minimal
    background check
Meanwhile Black and Brown people can't
walk through a neighborhood to buy candy, survive a routine
    traffic stop
without being murdered
No he wasn't trained in hills of Afghanistan
didn't learn bomb making techniques from the Taliban
It was here in America he learned apartheid policies
Separate and unequal
Separate schools
Separate bathrooms
Separate
Separate
Separate
that breed a rampant repressed homophobe
It was from demagogues like Trump

that purport building walls and keeping people
out and inciting fear fear fear
It was America and the Bush clan
that proved you could lie and kill and get away with it
that certain populations were disposable
I've seen these massacres before
it was when Black and Brown queers were dying rapidly of AIDS
only then the guns were indifference
Guns were in hands of every American
Guns were in hands of politicians
of doctors
in a system that hated queers
I've seen it before this killing
in the zig zag scars of women poets who died
of breast cancer
And institutions that still claim their legacy
Like many I've searched the hallways for justice
paced up and down
begged to be heard
asked for simple treatment
for simple problems
Gaslighted
Bankrupted
Run around
Only to find out in America
women's wombs are big business
I've seen this killing before
It happens every day
reality shows
teaching us to step on and crush
each other to get ahead

A television that shows someone actually slicing
Khaddafi's jugular
I've left so many places/communities
because of safety concerns
Sekou Sundiata died in the emergency room from a heart attack
Willie Ninja, that beautiful, beautiful dancer went blind
I could go on but my brother Essex Hemphill
is calling to me
telling me/us as he did in the crisis so long ago
telling us to wrap our arms around each other
and hold tight
Hold tight
Gently.

SURVIVOR

Contrary to popular opinion I never liked Diana Nyad
in my mind overrated white woman
ex-Olympic swimmer most recently swam from Cuba to Florida
privileged
thrill seeker
daredevil
doing voluntarily what so many POC
are forced to do while attempting to gain freedom
drowning in boats, falling overboard, terrible accidents,
falling into the jaws of sharks, those waters a meat fest
for predators, slavers.
Sometimes I think about slavery and think if only those waters
could tell the tale
I've always wanted to say to those people who go on the reality show
Survivor for kicks
try being an artist and make it your career choice
or how about a single mother or father trying to raise a family
on minimum wage living in an impoverished area
try being someone who comes to America and
doesn't speak the language whose entire survival rests upon
learning English
arriving in a strange land, on strange soil, estranged from everything
you have ever known

like hitting your head against a glass door, or mirrors
like optical illusions that used to be in the old fun houses
or how about being uninsured and being sick for a number
of years
weathering that storm
or insured but burdened with a costly illness
health plans don't cover
or like so many of my students who are bullied to the point
they have nowhere to turn and no longer have knowledge
of their own name.
No I never liked Diana Nyad
until one day I caught a clip of her on *Ellen*
I caught the part where she talked about her friendship
with Superman Christopher Reeve who in real life suffered
paralysis from the neck down.
He looked at her in later years after she'd retired from swimming
said he feared she wasn't living her own dreams, that
she was an Olympian
And something about her conversations with him motivated her
to try again, to listen.
Maybe through her I saw the frayed ends of my own unlived
    dreams,
my own fear that caused paralysis
And so by the end of that conversation with Ellen
where Diana talked about returning to her Olympic self
by swimming from Cuba to Florida at age sixty challenging
every notion of what it means to be an athlete, a woman,
and the stereotypes of aging I was crying
by the time she looked into the camera and said
Don't give up
Never give up your dreams.

CITIZEN

A friend and I were talking after Trump's election
She remarked in the words of MLK, "There are really two Americas."
In response, I say, "There are probably seven, eight, nine, ten,
   twenty Americas, more than we can count."
I know that during the early '90s during the early AIDS crisis, I saw
   another America
As Hilton Als says, when the bodies of dead gay men felled by AIDS
were being tossed out into the streets in garbage bags.
I had many friends who were sick.
I asked one guy, "What took so long with Medicare, why all the
   red tape?"
He said, "They are just waiting to see if I die first."
It felt as if someone dropped ice water on me
I was so shocked
But I remember the yellow green brown walls of Bellevue and St.
   Vincent's Hospital
wards full of sick skinny gay men
covered in lesions and purple spots like in leper colonies
In my recent experiences with the healthcare system
I was kept in the front offices of a doctor's office until I explained
I had fancy insurance
"Oh, why didn't you say so," he said.
Then I was led to a spare office in the back with a black leather couch

He pulled out a contract and was smiling so nice
So many times, I was sent to specialists who knew nothing
Once I gave my mother a computer, it broke somehow
and my dad not wanting to admit he knew nothing put the wires in
an impossible place.
I laughed, until I learned doctors do it, too.
Back in the day poet Hattie Gossett used to talk about the
    difference between
snow in Harlem and snow on the Upper East Side
Whereas in Harlem it wasn't plowed and left in icy mounds
Turned black with soot, urine, and feces
When I graduated college and first began my teaching career
I worked at a literacy center in Harlem attached to a public
    elementary school
It was there I saw two Americas
Whereas like in South Africa under apartheid
Black students were given Bantu education
forced to speak Afrikaans
I read a headline in a newspaper the other day that called
an opiod epidemic in a white American town heartbreaking
They didn't say the word heroin until much later and it said
    heartbreaking
Whereas I remember the crack epidemic in inner city Black
    neighborhoods
Some of which was planted to destroy them, and the people were
    called thugs,
addicts, menaces, thrown off welfare rolls
The war on drugs which is now admittedly a code for
the war against Black people
Rockefeller drug laws were invented to put immense numbers of
    POC

in jail for limited possession.
They got immeasurably long sentences and it was called anything
    but heartbreaking.
Given all that I have said
What if I told you that little smiley yellow emoticons
That all the texting and social media addicts use
are just masks
What if beneath them were war, savagery, rage, poverty, fear,
jealousy, envy, people fighting and
desperate to survive
After Trump was elected people on the left kept claiming
He's stolen our democracy
I would never dispute his evil and our world is forever changed
But I have to ask
Exactly what democracy is it we are speaking of?
Is it the one of slavery and subsequent 100 years of Jim Crow?
Is it the slaughter of Native American people
Treaties broken like today's voting machines in poor and Black
    neighborhoods?
Is it Standing Rock where a pipeline is driven through sacred
    Native lands,
People tear gassed arrested?
Is it the recent ICE detention centers, Brown people held for seeking
    asylum
and put in cages?
The millennium started with Bush's stolen election
Which democracy is it we are speaking of?
Is it the one that started relentless never-ending wars in Iraq and
    Afghanistan
With thousands of casualties?
Is it the democracy that dropped Napalm on people running

Skin burnt off
Is it the one where a woman was assaulted daily
dragged across the world stage
and her perpetrator became the leader of a supposedly free world?
What if I said after Trump's election
A veil lifted
And all we've lost are illusions
I don't know about Obama, but the only hope I have
is in two moments—
When he entered office, he carried a book of poetry by Derek Walcott.
He wanted the world to see poetry's importance.
Three months after he entered office
Obama boarded a plane to Ghana
He went to and was photographed at Cape Coast Castle, the
    former warehouse
Used for slaves
There Obama stood and looked onto the Atlantic.
He acknowledged slavery and the Middle Passage,
That's the hope I have.
There in the loving defiance of Black slaves
In the unsung
runaways, the escapees, prisoners, martyrs
Those who never made it out
And in my students, the teachers, their voices, their formation,
inspiration
Artists shaping the world from earth and water into clay

CIRCUS ACTS

All rage aside
I gotta hand it to Trump and his admin because they
really have managed to stage the greatest heist
and show on earth
Like the old Ringling Brothers and Barnum and Bailey Circus
used to boast trapeze and live animal acts
before animal rights activists shut them down
I mean, this is like the heists in *Oceans 11*, *12*, and *13*
I could never watch because they seemed so contrived
Yes, they have delivered something so spectacular
it's better than anything Karl Rove could have dreamt of
This even outdoes the architects of apartheid that turned the entire
   country
of South Africa into a jail for Black people
All I can think of is the movie *Gladiator* when Joaquin Phoenix plays
a corrupt emperor with no experience who
achieved power illicitly
When asked how he'd rule over the people
he said, "Give them games"
and every day slaves fill an arena to fight.
This is some high-wire sawed-in-half-lady shit
This is like some Hannah Arendt the banality of evil and
the bureaucratization of homicide shit

where the Holocaust was hidden in paperwork, menial tasks
everyone had a hand in
so no one saw the whole picture
I mean this is some sci-fi Octavia Butler and *The Hunger Games* shit
I mean nodding to Jayne Cortez's
poem describing the rape of Joanne Little
Asking just what the fuck was she supposed to do
Tongue his encrusted toilet stool lips
Suck the numbers off his tin badge
choke on his clap trap balls
Squeeze the nub of his rotten maggots
Sing god bless America thank you
fucking my life away?

This is some scrambling around
too many balls in air
can't keep track shit
More buttons pushed than when trapped in
an elevator panic
Some through the roof ratings shit
Record-breaking *Roots* shit
For pleasure, I watch the sci-fi spoof *Agents of Shield*
on Netflix
An agency of superheroes seeking justice
One of the characters said like the real-life Mark Zuckerberg
We no longer have to surveil people because
they offer up their information for free.
When alone, just to myself I secretly call Facebook/Racebook
Can't say it out loud to anyone because you know . . .
people steal.
One of my friends, an older white woman who took the hit

for Abbie Hoffman
She went to prison.
She said, "Everything there is racialized,
they play movies constantly that will divide and create groups."
That's what happens on Facebook.
We are constantly fed race stories
whipped up into frenzies
It like a civil war every day.
This is some deep shit shit.
Talking to one of my students and
they said, "Oh Trump's so stupid,"
I started to yell, "That's what they want us to believe."
"He's playing the character in a soap opera
And we experience him as a character we know."
Years ago, I was asked to join panel for an academic discussion
on Beyoncé
I asked that we not consider her as a personality but as a business
Like a marketing machine
Every time a Hollywood celebrity wants to sell something
these days they say something shocking with regard to race and gender.
Singer John Mayer referred to his dick publicly as a white supremacist.
The Seinfeld guy was filmed in a club, responding to a Black heckler
and said something like, "You're lucky you're not hanging from a tree
with a fork up your ass."
The Seinfeld box set was released the next day and sold millions of
    copies.
The day before Madonna's album dropped she took to Twitter
referred to her Black son as, "My Nigga."
It's all a strategy like when Jay and Bey sampled the lines
preceding an infamous beating of Tina Turner by Ike on their
    album,

115

It said, "Eat the cake Anna Mae,"
referring to when Ike brutally shoved food into Tina's mouth.

From the beginning, you could tell Trump was running on
a racist platform during the debates, everyone in his family
except Melania
died their hair platinum blonde and he made Hitleresque signals
to depict the Aryan race.
On the panel where I posited Bey and our reaction to her
as a business and result of clever marketing
there was great uproar and pushback by Black women
soon to graduate.
I don't care if you like me, I said,
but there has to be
analysis.

BLACK PANTHER

I watched *Black Panther*
and all I could think of was oh no
Giving permission
for a new crop of Black Americans
to visit Ghana and West Africa
Saying things like I'm home
and giving the Wakanda salute
Since Africa was presented as so easy
Bite-sized McNugget friendly
Lion King chunks
Some Africans would welcome them
but others would laugh
Big lumbering dumb Americans
Like those speaking English loud in foreign places
Swimming naked in religious communities
because the world is their oyster
I was embarrassed by it
Humbly asking someone to pardon our naïveté or privilege
It's not our fault we were brainwashed and estranged
I felt protective, too
remembering my trip to Ghana
The castle
Sitting at the edge of the ocean

Bathing
Where the ships were loaded
Walking through those dungeons
of unspeakable horror
Slaves standing knee deep
In feces and urine
Fishing food from waste
I wanted to protect what I saw there
Not wanting loud Black American tourists
with their soles walking all over the ground
At the slavery museum in Portugal
the guard explained to me
Most people don't even know what this is
Even after we explain, he said
Black Americans are the worst
Come straight from the ocean
won't wipe their dirty feet
ask where the whips and chains are
because they only want gore
I want to say there are some things the movie did well
I held back tears when I saw the cloth
The kente brought back memories
of my ancestral journey
The longing for home
When the young man travels through a portal
to the ancestral realm
There was beauty
I also knew well the storyline
The lost orphaned African American returning to Africa
It was my MFA thesis work
inspired by my trip to Ghana

And actually the scholarship didn't belong solely
to Ta-Nehisi Coates
It was Sadiya Hartman who wrote the book, *Lose Your Mother*
I was shocked that a superhero film
would attempt the depth of subject
But it quickly turned into using Africa as a backdrop for
African American identity issues
I was offended, too
All I could think of was Safiya Bukhari
a Black Panther and political prisoner
dead at 53
And what was done to Fred Hampton
and Huey Newton
I wanted to scream at the film, This isn't a revolution
They said with the merchandising it made billions
A cartoon, while our education healthcare neighborhood
are still lacking.
I thought other things too how it descended haplessly
into Black-on-Black war
and the CIA agent is a good guy
And female Black action figures
hadn't been seen on screen for forty years
Since the days of blaxploitation
And the same in literature
Thirty years between a prominent political
Artist lesbian
Like Audre Lorde
So actually, where's the progress?

MASK

I knew and I wrote years ago
that the entire sci-fi genre had changed
when at the end of one of the *Planet of the Apes* sagas
Caesar the talking ape responds to his white owner who infantilized
   him
On Caesar's rise to the throne
he says, Come home Caesar
Caesar responds of earth and America,
I am home
I knew that was a nod to the Obama age,
the first Black man in the White House
But it tipped the genre on its head
when every alien before and after says they want to return home
and Caesar says defiantly,
I am home
No longer a native son
no longer the space alien or stolen African
In my MFA thesis work long before the new *Apes* movie
I placed the character of Caesar at the mouth of Cape Coast Castle
following a trail of body parts spread across the Atlantic
trying to find his people
For Caesar to say you must acknowledge us
Another seminal moment was when Robert Downey, Jr. said

to a shocked audience, I am Iron Man
That was the end of the masked Superhero
A secret identity people would risk their lives to hide and discover
I remember feeling uncomfortable not knowing how Marvel would
   resolve
something we'd been so accustomed to
But I also knew and it's something I write often, how after 9/11
All Hollywood endings changed
In the film *Ladder 49* actor Joaquin Phoenix who plays a firefighter
doesn't emerge from the flames and it's devastating
Something you might have only witnessed in some dystopian sci-fi
I've been watching the TV show *Black Lightning*
A Black comic-book hero who's
trying to save a disenfranchised devastated Black community like
   Flint
or any urban ghetto anywhere that's been experimented upon
Drug ravaged whom the city wants to control
The only hope is Black Lightning
who is also a high school principal trying
to uplift the race
It's corny as hell
with low production values
And the evil man is so sadistic
it makes me wince
But the show gets interesting with *Black Lightning's*
two daughters who are also said to possess powers
the eldest teen is a lesbian
With lots of girl-on-girl action
The story gets interesting about ten episodes in
when his best friend the police chief
figures out who Lightning is and confronts him

I mean it should have been so obvious early on
It was ridiculous they didn't know
But I wasn't ready at all
when Black Lightning unmasked himself
His face naked before his friend
I felt his vulnerability
Raw powerlessness of being seen
Face wind eyes exposed
maybe it's because we've always cloaked ourselves
historically
Made friends with night fall
Dawoud Bey showing the Underground Railroad at night
Utter blackness silver purple
Blue hue shades
DuBois Dunbar
A Black student reciting "We Wear the Mask"
Contemporary times teach you to hate
fear the woods and nature
The setting for horror
But for Black people
it is freedom
Maybe that's why I winced
when he lifted his mask
Feeling both breath
and danger.

PROPHECY

Having been to Ghana twice, in 2005 and 2006,
the first time for almost a month and the second for two weeks,
a third time I traveled to South Africa in 2011
I could never call myself an expert on Africa, nor want to.
I can say that those trips changed my life forever, in mostly positive
  ways.
Based on those trips to Ghana and South Africa, I was able to predict
this moment in America where we would be obsessed with all
  things African
in art and film and culture.
I know when I saw the swirl of brown faces in Accra, experienced
  the bustling city
the stalls and stalls of vendors in Makola Market in Accra
and in Kumasi
and cell phones everywhere
I knew I was seeing gems of a hidden world/
with expanses of land, people, and innovation.
All I could say when I returned, as some white American tech giants
are starting to say now, "Africa is the frontier."
"Africa will decide our future."
I saw a similar but a different story in South Africa, a still burgeoning
and powerful queer and feminist community,

Innovation, business, art, and ideas that sprung up and bloomed
     after apartheid
I knew again Africa was the beginning and will be the end, alpha
     and omega.
After years of being crushed, colonized, raped, ravaged, and
pillaged by dictatorships, superpowers, colonialism, and tribal wars,
Africa is rising.
I saw it with my own eyes.
Five years ago I was hospitalized at NYU for about five days.
I had a series of kidney infections which some doctors were
     denying.
Only one believed me and treated me accordingly with proper
     antibiotics.
He was South Asian, he had trained at Mass General in Boston,
     where I'm from.
He was sitting on my bed in the penthouse since I had great
     insurance—people who are on death's door don't even get those
     kinds of rooms. It overlooked New York City.
I only had one other visitor, a white girl from my art therapy
     group, and the doctor.
After many years of strife and illness I was in an emotional wilderness
but I was talking to the doctor about books and writing and my
     travels in Africa.
I said, "It's the frontier."
He said, "Yes. I think China knows that and it's why they've
     invested so heavily there."

A second instance when I detailed my vision about Africa as the
     future—
It was sometime after I'd left Ghana. I was serving on an artist
     grant panel in New York and artists from Europe were being

considered but African artists, specifically one from Nigeria, was dismissed as being too far away.

I went home that night and prepared a speech to deliver to the committee.

I practiced in the mirror for the next day.

In one line I said, "It is time for us to consider African artists." My voice was trembling.

I was the one Black person on the panel, the one who represented diversity.

A lot was at stake. I don't remember the outcome but the person in me who had been to Ghana knew that it should never not be discussed,

that it should not be considered the dark unknown foreign continent ever again.

I'm sure my identity would have changed even more if I had stayed in Ghana.

I got involved with a young African man and saw a tiny bit of Africa through his eyes.

To be sure there's a mask he wore, one that's worn for Americans/ Black Americans

so that the ways and secrets of their culture are hidden, but through traveling with him

and experiencing some things through his eyes, Africa got into my bones

like the souls of all those slaves jailed and buried at Cape Coast and Elmina Castle.

Maybe it was like in a movie where ghosts have a message for the living.

They spoke to me and I carried their message forward.

This new awareness I had of Africa made its way into my lesson plans and my stories.

Ten years ago it was still uncommon in academia outside of African
    Studies to acknowledge Africa but as a Professor I brought it
    up in many lessons whether I was teaching Communications,
    Writing, or Solo Performance.
I think in small ways I was able to enact change.
Like the Black nurse from Nigeria who had no interest in Nigeria.
I ran into her years later and she said, "Because of you I took my
    daughters home to Nigeria. I learned the importance of knowing
    where I come from."
She might have been part of the team of Black nurses I took to the
    African burial ground in downtown Manhattan/steps from the
    9/11 Museum.
One woman immediately got the spirit and started to cry-laugh,
another wrote of how the bones of African slaves spoke to her.
In another class a young Black woman from Sierra Leone talked
    about how
her family fled the Civil War and her mother saw a neighbor's
    decapitated head
posted on a fence by soldiers as a warning sign.
In another scenario two boys in a city school who were both from
    Africa
bonded together and created a presentation on Africa.
They were proud and I knew it was because I gave them safe space.
There was one mixed-race young man in another class whose
    family fled Uganda.
He came out as gay in my class and said, "In my country I could be
    killed for who I am."
Even though he was often absent and didn't receive a good grade
He knew I was a writer and when leaving said, "Please publish
    your stories, Miss."
Africa changed my creative work and poems.

I can never not think of Cape Coast
I can never not stop wanting to go
to visit
to see
to remember
to bathe at Cape Coast
or ride fishing boats at Elmina
or wander along beaches of Benin
Or go to South Africa and stare at the beauty of Table Mountain
and its twelve apostles and the role the landscape played in
inspiring prisoners on Robben Island to end apartheid
All of this to say, I am by no means an expert but last month
I volunteered at a gallery where thousands of visual artists donate
their work to a fair once a year.
Every year at the very end I notice the works and images of Black
people remain.
It's not conscious but all the work by white artists is coveted and
purchased.
This year a giant sculpture of a brown vagina with hair remained.
I immediately purchased it, and loved it.
I continued looking around and I noticed in a corner a tiny red,
black, and green sculpture of the African continent.
I picked it up and said to myself, "I must have this piece."
"It would be wrong to leave it here."
I got home and opened the box and there was a note from a proud
African artist living in Brooklyn.
She said to the unknown purchaser, "Africa is rising."
I imagine somewhere in this story, in my journeys, is a metaphor
for me.
I, too, like Africa, am rising.

BORN FREES

I used to always write about Assotto Saint
Slamming his hand down on the pulpit at Donald Woods's funeral
when it was common to hide the cause of death of
young men who'd died from AIDS
if they were buried at all and weren't abandoned
Someone told me about a thin boy
thin with fear and death
played piano for the choir
no one touched him
or talked about it
I know in my mother's family
her mother's sister said a parasite
had killed her son when he died suddenly
But I remember once him coming out of a gay bar in Boston
all the white boys said, "How do you know her?"
I don't know if he or I said cousin
I'm his cousin
He made me promise not to tell anyone in the family
I'd seen him there
So when they said parasite I knew something didn't ring true
His mother, a seemingly healthy woman, died shortly after that
but I always felt their deaths were related
His mother either from the lies or repression
or a broken heart
having lost her young son

And I know everyone blames Jussie Smollett for his lies and staged
   attack
but it makes me think there was something very toxic going on
that he didn't feel he could talk to someone
Either that he was covering up
an addiction or a hookup.
Watching Assotto stand up at Donald's funeral and tell the truth
goes down in history as one of the bravest moments I'd ever
   witnessed
Either that or Audre Lorde spreading open the arms of her dashiki
the bravest woman we'd all witnessed
telling a crowded room of followers,
"I began on this journey as a coward."
That or seeing a friend at the height of the AIDS era
at a bar his face covered in purple welts
refusing to hide
going out in public
That or Donald Woods being feeble
barely able to walk
accepting an award as a director of AIDS films
Or an ex-lover on a beach taking off her top
and refusing to hide her mastectomy scar
Or when Danitra Vance performed at The Public Theater
and danced naked revealing her mastectomy scars
and Audre refusing to wear a prosthesis
Or when Zakes Mokae in *Master Harold and the Boys* in the first
   Broadway play
that a cousin took me to
said to his white master, "Have you ever seen a Black man's ass?"
and pulled down his pants and revealed himself to the audience
I was sixteen years old
Or seeing my mother beaten religiously

and still go out to work as if it hadn't happened at all
Or even me surviving so many
incredible tests
Once when I was talking to a doctor, I doubted my strength
He looked at me incredulously and said, "You are strong."
Another doctor looked at me
my suffering
And asked, "Isn't anyone there for you?"
And another said, "You deserve to be taken care of."
Today once more I am nursing my broken heart
Caused by someone who betrayed
was not honest
That and attending an event and asking white people to give up
their seats to Black people who couldn't sit down
And seeing social justice in action
Yes I often think of Assotto for the important place
he resides in my history
But today I am examining his tactics
pulling the tools off the shelf
dusting off the weaponry
in an exhibit
because today I need to use what he taught me.

Today I feel that puff of rage
That continuous assault
And I want to stand up and testify
though I, too, haven't been asked
I want to interrupt all the proceedings
all the places Black lesbians
have been erased
and silenced

Like looking down at a manuscript
seeing that they asked a young white woman to write about
Black queer history
when it's been my area of expertise
forever
Or only attributing '80s and '90s AIDS activism
To ACT UP
I want the point of outrage now to not only the historicizing of AIDS
But the fact that women and Black lesbians
have been erased from the dialogue
When there were so many organizations like GMAD
Other Countries ADODI
Men of All Colors Together
Salsa Soul/AAlUSC
Las Buenas Amigas
and more
Or asking where are all the Black lesbians on *Pose*
because certainly they were on the piers and part of that history
And why are white men constantly at the helm
to tell our stories
And why don't white queers recognize this
That and seeing panel after panel being organized on history and art
all things important to the world and no one thinking or noticing
it might be important to have a Black lesbian present
Just like they kicked Stormé out of
the Stonewall narrative.
And what about the people who weren't on the streets
but in jobs
fighting the system
The dykes and queers meeting each other forming community
and connections and families

and love
Just like in South Africa where they prevented intermingling
but ways were found
And each time we touched or loved
found each other in darkness and light
It was resistance
Each time we told each other you're beautiful
You're not wrong
It was resistance
When we stood up to the parents and families
and courts and those that shunned us
It was resistance
Wore what we really wanted
It was resistance
Yelled at doctors and drug professionals
It was resistance
Every time we wrote and read poems
It was resistance
Every time some queer kid
stays alive because they saw us
read us
discovered the archive
We've won
Every war is fought on our bodies
And one day after the gender racial
sexual orientation wars are over
in America
there will be a new generation
just like in South Africa called
the Born Frees.

A NEW STORY

I SHOULD HAVE KNOWN from the start there'd be trouble when we were listening to a song, she started to twerk and said, "I'll be Rhianna and you be Drake."

"Drake?! I'm never Drake. Drake doesn't do anything he just stands there and folds his arms!" I said it was telling that she saw herself as the star and me her back-up dancer. It was a way of rendering me invisible but maybe I don't need to say that. I want to write a story about being trapped in a story.

I see myself as a mime, one you see outdoors with the sad white painted face appearing with hands to scale a wall or like they are trapped in a box somehow. Someone asks, "What's wrong?" and the mime turns to a sign: "Help I'm trapped in a story."

Sometimes it's my own story that I repeat over and over my patterns, my past, my getting involved with people who render me invisible, people who make me part of their background, and it doesn't quite matter what my story is, but the purpose of this is my frustration with myself at repeating my own story, how many times I peer outside of the box to see there's a new story, possibly a new beginning, freedom but I'm trapped in my own story. I see it in their eyes when they are talking to me, and it's a story but very rarely is it my story. It's their story. It's inaccurate and they become enraged at me for the story they've told themselves about me, and I see them kicking and punching at the ghost they've created, the monster in their story.

And it's my dream that if this were a movie or a music video or something one day I'll get a speaking part. One day, I'll be able to participate in my own story or the one that's told about me.

One day I'll have a conversation
or someone will stop to have a conversation with me
not the person they've made
but the person I am
and I'll get to live outside the box
And all those untold stories in me
all those bruises
all those suppressions
lack of being able to participate
have landed in my belly
and turned to rot
and it's always so small and confining and I can't get away because
    it's their story and it's like a noose around my neck pulled tight
    my feet dangling in air.
I'm liking some of the preachers these days
where they posit the possibility of a new world
one lived in spirit
Not living in the constant matrix
of fear, doubt, lack, limitation, not-enoughness
Like a ping pong back and forth
greed envy
our daily bread.

I don't want to leave you there so I am creating a new mantra for
    myself.
Say it with me:
I am going to write a new story.
I am going to write a new story.

MARKED SAFE

FOR STONEWALL 50

I want to thank the maestro Tim Gunn,
Heidi Klum, also every episode of *Project Runway* and *Runway
   All-Stars*,
Every gay and lesbian contestant that ever sewed, stitched sequins
   to dresses
or pantaloons
every queer who ever threw a tantrum, walked out and came back
   to win.
Thank you to the Jersey and Atlanta Housewives and spin-offs
To all their queer queen besties
I want to thank RuPaul and every queen on every episode of *Drag
   Race*
Also, that dollar store cashier I ran into with my mother in small-
   town Massachusetts
who actually thought I was RuPaul and kept calling me, "Miss
   Honey."
Thank you, Oprah, her close friend designer Nate Berkus.
I extend condolences to the lover he lost when the tsunami hit Sri
   Lanka.
I also want to thank Walmart and the trans person who worked
behind the register when my mother worked there as a greeter.

When eventually she was fired for wearing women's clothes,
to my shock, my mother said, "That's unjust and I think it's
    discrimination."
I want to thank that person wherever they are.
I want to thank that mixed-race lesbian Josie on *Top Chef*
I want to thank every LGBTQIA person on every show that my
    mother
watched religiously, because each and every one of them
in one way or another
prepared my mother at eighty-four years old for the queer art
    catalogue I was a part of
that I brought home to show her called *Cast of Characters.*
Holding my breath, I handed it to her, asked her to guess of all the
    images
which was mine.
She saw the word *queer* first, "Why do you call yourselves that?
    That's
like saying you're Niggers."
I tried to explain the concept of reclaiming language used against us.
My mother refused to listen.
She thumbed through the images, eyes wide with wonder.
She knows I don't usually show her stuff for many reasons.
She gave her opinion on each image.
"Ooooh this one with flowers," she pointed. "I like this."
The next was an image of a man with cock and balls out,
"I don't like this one," she said.
She persisted onto the next image.
"Pregnant butch," she said out loud and giggled.
"A pregnant butch," she said again as if fascinated by the idea.
"I don't see yours, oh but here it is!"

She fastened on a blue and red watercolor of figures gathered in
   grief
titled, *6 times*.
"It's the family of Stephon Clark," I explained. "That Black kid
   from Sacramento
police shot in the back six to eight times, unarmed in his backyard.
They said he was a burglar."
"I wanted to paint the pictures of his family grieving because they
   had no voice
and were made invisible."
My mother got quiet, mouthed something like a ha
Her eyes narrowed and full, like when I visit and we watch shows
about slavery together/like in *Roots* when Chicken George has to
   leave his
son at the crossroads to gain freedom.
My mother wants to cry but doesn't.
She commands me to show the catalogue to my father.
Later she asks to take a picture because she wants to show my
ninety-year-old aunt.

In New York this year we are celebrating,
The 50th anniversary of the Stonewall Riots.
My queer friends complain about all the festivities as
"The monster that ate New York,"
But I say I'm excited by it all
If only because I can go home to my family
(Because of all of those queens and kings before me)
Marked safe.

WHEN THE RAINBOW IS ENUF

FOR NTOZAKE SHANGE

The internet has transformed our grieving patterns
Everything comes and goes so quickly
After death there's a tremendous outpouring and then a few
weeks later months years later nothing
I have come now to watch all who shaped me die
Never got to write about or even register Prince
Then Aretha
Ntozake
People without whom I couldn't have formed my voice
My identity
I joke now there's probably not a Black girl alive who came through
a theater program in the United States who hadn't encountered
the work of Ntozake Shange
In fact, I know some University Theater Programs ban *For Colored
  Girls*
from being performed "Choose something else," they say
because it's been performed so much
I chuckle thinking about how many times Ntozake's words were
used by Black girls as audition monologues for a theater
"And I will be presenting the lady in green/or the lady in yellow"

And then them skipping around the room talking about Toussaint
	Louveture
Or the infamous somebody almost walked off with all of my stuff
Or if they were really dramatic they might perform the lady in red
with the perils of Beau Willie Brown, a crazed Vietnam Vet
and that infamous last line
About how he dropped the kids out of the window
In our college production, I was the lady in blue
a character that was rather obscure in compare to the others
I remember the beginning of the choreopoem playing
childhood games and then being frozen while a woman came around
and tagged us awake "I'm outside Houston . . . "
"I'm outside Chicago . . . "
And "this is for colored girls who've considered suicide/but moved to
the ends of their own rainbows"
The play was such that you could memorize everyone else's lines
I struggled initially with how to pronounce Ntozake's name
and read her Black vernacular and slash mark punctuation
But it was like reading Morrison's *Beloved* which I tried at least five
	times before
I understood but then the codes gave way to an ecstasy and
	understanding
Her words became mine
Even though I was a young suburb girl
And the kinds of male partner violence that Ntozake spoke of was
	foreign to me
Later in a conversation at her house she remarked she didn't want
older women to perform *For Colored Girls*
As the words became too bitter in their mouths
A point we starkly disagreed on

But 'Zake's words were the first to unlock an experience in
    literature
A pool, a mirror by which Black girls could see themselves
like Tubman
She freed a lot of souls
That said, she was a hero of mine
And so when I first had the chance to meet her
as an adult many many years after undergrad
I was honored and floored
A friend of mine from Boston managed her
I went to meet her at Nuyorican Poets Café
It was after her second stroke
And she was dancing with her hands and hair
Her arms were raised above her head and she moved wildly to the
    music
her dreadlocks with gold beads moved with her
Afterward we hugged and were like old friends or sisters
I saw her many times after that
Once she came to see me perform
And I couldn't believe I was performing for the woman who'd
    given me words
that was a beautiful moment when my mentor became an equal
I don't think I could ever impart what she's meant
but I will always remember her
after two strokes
with her hands over her head
raised to the sky god
Dancing.

A TALE OF TWO PANDEMICS

The headline in yesterday's news blared A Tale of Two Pandemics
Shocking Inequities in the Healthcare System
what got me was use of words *shocking* and *two*
Those of us who lived through through the 1980s early '90s AIDS
   crisis already knew about the existence of two New Yorks
Two twenty thirty forty fifty Americas maybe more
Depending on age race class citizenship status
Entirely different systems for those who aren't white straight
middle class
Those of us who saw our brothers friends sisters die at the hands of
   system that shunned
Refused to treat
Threw away the unwanted
Still can't forget a gay friend waiting
For Medicaid to treat HIV
He got sicker and sicker.
I asked why Medicaid took so long
He said they're waiting to see if I'll die first
That wasn't the America I learned about in elementary school
I was instructed to put my hand over heart
and salute
That wasn't the free America we sang of
People who are LGBTQIA already know there are two Americas

A doctor who kept forcing me to take a pregnancy test
Even after I insisted at the time
I only have sex with women
I saw his scorn/still a test
He made me pay for
And those women who were forcibly sterilized
Had wombs their life force taken
Left dry barren by doctors
who never even stopped to explain
Felt entitled to take scar women's bodies
Breasts cut off no options or consolation given
Women who aren't rich and white already know invisible lines you
    can't cross
With no insurance or Medicaid
Forced into black markets for drugs
A land of botched care botched procedures
Black people already know
separate doors
separate entrances
treatments
options
Existing long after Jim Crow
And I have kept waiting for this moment
This time of a medical #MeToo
When those who've suffered from botched procedures and the
    indignities
Step out from shadows
Speak and name the atrocities committed
medical malpractice
I won't blame all doctors
some are good

just middlemen like so many in a broken system doing what they can
and I'm grateful for the good ones in this pandemic risking
their own lives
But the image of medical researchers that we see in movies and on
   television who understand a complex problem
pour through medical books and science journals
Stay up all night burning midnight oil to find a cure
Who weep with concern
are mostly false
rare like ones who find cures
and refuse to patent
or personally profit
Those days have become myth
what's replaced them are businessmen
wanting status amongst peers
entry to country clubs and power
Gaslighters hustlers actors like Trump
There is a doctor at Mount Sinai
star of his field
charged with drugging and raping his patients
No one believed til it was proven
his victims
were only Black women
the rest he left alone.

I CAN'T BREATHE

I suppose I should place them under separate files
Both died from different circumstances kind of, one from HIV/
   AIDS and possibly not having taken his medicines
the other from COVID-19 coupled with
complications from an underlying HIV status
In each case their deaths may have been preventable if one had
   taken his meds and the hospital had thought to treat the other
instead of sending him home saying, He wasn't sick enough
he died a few days later
They were both mountains of men
dark Black beautiful gay men
both more than six feet tall fierce and way ahead of their time
One's drag persona was Wonder Woman and the other started a
   Black fashion magazine
He also liked poetry
They both knew each other from the same club scene we all grew up in
When I was working the door at a club one frequented
He would always say to me, "Haven't they figured out you're a star yet?"
And years ago bartending with the other when I complained about
   certain people and treatment he said, "Sounds like it's time for
   you to clean house."
Both I know were proud of me the poet star stayed true to my roots
I guess what stands out to me is that they both were

gay Black mountains of men
Cut down
Felled too early
And it makes me think the biggest and blackest are almost always
more vulnerable
My white friend speculates why the doctors sent one home
If he had enough antibodies
Did they not know his HIV status
She approaches it rationally
removed from race as if there were any rational for sending him home
Still she credits the doctors for thinking it through
But I speculate they saw a big Black man before them
Maybe they couldn't imagine him weak
Maybe because of his size color class they imagined him strong
said he's okay
Which happened to me so many times
Once when I'd been hospitalized at the same time as a white girl
she had pig-tails
we had the same thing but I saw how tenderly they treated her
Or knowing so many times in the medical system I would never
have been treated so terribly if I had had a man with me
Or if I were white and entitled enough to sue
Both deaths could have been prevented both were almost first to
fall in this season of death
But it reminds me of what I said after Eric Garner a large Black
man was strangled to death over some cigarettes
Six cops took him down
His famous last words were I can't breathe
and now George Floyd
so if we are always the threat
To whom or where do we turn for protection?

WHY I CLING TO FLOWERS

I was trying to think of what it means
why I keep painting and posting flowers and trees in the pandemic
I know they're beautiful
And they assert amidst any chaos and confusion
Life on the planet
Every spring
Despite climate change every natural disaster
Purple crocus push up out of the ground determined
I'm fascinated by their colors striped purple violet and white
Red blue and yellow
I love that some humans place wire nets over them to protect their
    growth
so they don't get trampled on
I sometimes think of Brooklyn streets as fashion runways
All the flowers model for humans trying to look their best
in various poses showing off their blooms
Each trying to outdo the other with fabulousness
Like Black women on Easter
wearing an array of hats
I love pink purple magenta magnolia blossoms
How each bulb occupies a separate branch looking and pointing to
    the sky like an elegant candelabra
I love the daffodils red orange yellow faces

and one daffodil that I pass each day pushes its neck through
an opening in a metal garden gate
I identify with how it breaks apart
stands separate
As if refusing confines of a cell
I struggle to understand what this all means
Why I cling to flowers
When the newsfeed reports COVID-19 death after death
and fear
They say the pandemic most affects Black people migrant workers
    and poor Brown people globally, the aged and those with
    underlying conditions
And your friends are still dying from AIDS even when you thought
    hoped and prayed the worst was over
They say the next two weeks will be the pandemic's greatest peak
    in America
People are yelling and fighting
in grocery stores
on the street
there is so much fear
And the life you knew good or bad may never return
But finally talking to my father today I
understood my connection to flowers more
Over the years, anticipating his demise he's given me messages
Said, You've never given me any problems
You went off and did things on your own
You did everything all by yourself
You decided to go to New York and never looked back
You've made it on your own.
Today we are talking about the pandemic
I try to find masks and hand sanitizer to send to my family

Touched and impressed by my efforts, my father said
You still look out for us
You're a beautiful girl
I'm glad you're my daughter
I am here for you
And then I understand what it all means
If we can survive
have equipment means money
support conditions
There are also other possibilities
We can heal.

ACKNOWLEDGMENTS

Greatest thanks and heartfelt love and gratitude to Amy Scholder, for vision, belief, agenting, editing, and helping to bring this book to fruition.

Great thanks to Elaine Katzenberger for her work, support, and saying Yes. Many thanks also to Stacey Lewis at City Lights for all her work, and to everyone at City Lights.

Many thanks to Natasha Shapiro, Karen Finley, Gregg Bordowitz, Kyle Dacuyan, Nicole-Dennis Benn, Claudia Rankine, Sarah Schulman, Erica Cardwell, Tommy Pico, Avram Finkelstein, Dorothy Allison, Eric Pliner, and Jonathan Bloom, Alisa Yalan, Jenny Keyser, Matthew Buckingham, and Anselm Berrigan at *The Brooklyn Rail*.

Shout-outs to Jane Ursula Harris, Shelley Marlow, Ellen Goldin, Sur Rodney Sur, Zach Seeger, Tom Gilroy, Franklin Furnace, and Denniston Hill.

PHOTO BY PATRICIA SILVA

ABOUT THE AUTHOR

POET, PROFESSOR, AND PERFORMER, Pamela Sneed is the author of *Sweet Dreams, Kong,* and *Imagine Being More Afraid of Freedom than Slavery.* She was a Visiting Critic at Yale, and at Columbia University's School of the Arts, and is online faculty at Chicago's School of the Art Institute teaching Human Rights and Writing Art. She also teaches new genres at Columbia's School of the Arts in the Visual Dept. Her work is widely anthologized and appears in Nikki Giovanni's, *The 100 Best African American Poems.*